Who *Are* These People

Books by Cassandra Foster

For Young People

A Good Story: A Collection of Short Short Stories

Do You Know Us? A Collection of Short Stories

Cassandra Foster is the author of two books targeted to juveniles. Both books were supported in part by the DC Commission on the Arts and Humanities, an agency supported in part by the National Endowment for the Arts. She holds Ph.D. and MS degrees in computational linguistics from Georgetown University and a BA degree from Howard University, both in Washington, DC. She is an avid tournament bridge player. She is enthusiastic about her grandchildren and children.

Who *Are* These People

A Story about Bridge Players in the Washington Bridge Unit

Cassandra Foster

Who *Are* These People. Copyright © 2006 by Mildred C. Smith

ISBN-13 Soft Cover 978-0-9778641-2-6

First Printing 2008

Printed in the United States of America

To My Children and Grandchildren

Acknowledgements

Where would I be without you on my side, God?

Thanks to Christine Lam for the cover design and book layout.

Table of Contents

The Story behind the Stories

This book contains stories about African American men and women. They all turned at least 80 years old by May 1, 2008. They have in common membership in a duplicate bridge club—the Washington Bridge Unit where they play the card game bridge. The book contains several stories, with one story for each subject or married couple.

The stories are based on taped interviews of the subjects made between May 1, 2007 and May 16, 2008. To help with the time perspective, the date of the interview is at the end of each story. The location point of view is Washington, DC.

These people are the trailblazers. They have worked hard. You will find that most of these persons are still active in competitive tournament bridge. Most are currently church members, and most are still quite active in the church. Many are voracious readers, travel extensively, and have other hobbies. They appear youthful and healthy. They are close to their families.

The stories in the book tell about the lives of the subjects—when and where they were born, where they grew up, their careers, their families, their struggles, and their philosophies of life. There are pictures of the subjects. The stories include how bridge was introduced into their lives and how they came to be members of the Washington Bridge Unit. Keeping with the bridge tradition, these stories discuss the subjects using their first names.

Not only will the reader learn about the lives of the subjects in the book, but also there are interesting parallels in many of the stories about the culture of the US during a certain period. For example, many of the subjects who worked and lived in the south often went north to New York City to pursue advanced college degrees.

The Washington Bridge Unit (WBU) is a unit in the Mid-Atlantic Section (MAS) of the American Bridge Association (ABA). In fact, WBU and MAS were forming members of the ABA. The ABA formed in the 1930s. African Americans could not participate at that time in the predominant bridge organization in the US, the American Contract Bridge League or ACBL. ABA came about to fill that void. The stories use either the full name of the bridge organizations or their more commonly used abbreviated forms--WBU, ABA, ACBL.

The appendix contains a partial organizational structure of the ABA and the questionnaire used as a basis for the interviews. The names of many bridge personalities can be found in *Defining Moments: A 70 Year Chronicle of the American Bridge Association* and ACBL's *The Official Encyclopedia of Bridge.*

Mildred Anderson

This is the story of Mildred Anderson. Mildred is the consummate bridge player. Since the age of nine, her major joy and preoccupation have been the game of bridge. She was born on December 31, 1922 in Macon Georgia. She was an only child. It was in Macon that she obtained most of her education. She attended Ballard Normal School for grades 6 through 12. For college she received a degree from Georgia State College and a degree from Beda Etta College. As you will see, this story will include bridge throughout since it has been such a major part of Mildred's life.

During the summers when she was a child, Mildred's mother would send her to visit her aunt and cousins rather than to summer camp. Her aunt would assign chores to the children before leaving for work. Since Mildred was staying with them, she was included in the chores. The children played bridge, and the two persons who lost and were not sitting at the bridge table had to get up and do the work. Mildred's mother did not make her work when she was at home, and she did not want to work. So she had to win, but she did not know how to play bridge that summer when she was nine years old. She remembers telling her cousins that her mother did not make her work at home. Her cousins told her if she stayed there, she was either going to work or learn to play bridge. The cousins taught her, and she learned quickly.

Back at home Mildred's parents did not know she could play bridge. Her mother played bridge, and she discovered Mildred could play accidentally. She was hosting her bridge club, and one of the ladies was sick. Mildred volunteered to play the hand. Her mother told her she did not know anything about cards. The other ladies convinced Mildred's mother to let her sit there and pretty much be dummy. Mildred sat there and proceeded to win.

After finishing college in Macon, Mildred taught school for about four years. She then wanted to attend Howard University. So, she set out for Washington, DC. Because of racial segregation and discrimination in Macon, Mildred was happy to leave. She stayed in the dormitory at Howard University, and it was on that campus that she met her husband. She says it was almost love at first sight. A friend of her future husband looked at Mildred with interest, but her husband (to be) told his friend, "No, she is mine." That proved to be true, and they were married for 24 years when they divorced in 1974. Mildred thinks her devotion to bridge probably affected their relationship. She was involved with bridge with gusto, but her husband, who became a dentist, did not play. Mildred says the divorce did not bother her. She used bridge as a substitute, and she loved a life in bridge.

In the meanwhile Mildred was developing a serious bridge routine. She played bridge in the dormitories, often after lights were out. She became a member of a party bridge game that met every other Saturday night. There were usually three tables of bridge in play. After doing that for two or three years, she began duplicate bridge in 1957. She recalls that a WBU member, Ola Parks, introduced her to duplicate. Mildred recalls that because she loved bridge so much, she became president of the Carver Girls women's duplicate bridge club in which she played. She remembers Iris Carr as one of the club members. She says it was a nice big club for women, and she got to know Iris and lots of other women. She remained a member of the club until she became inactive in the WBU. Mildred was also secretary of the WBU for two two-year terms. She was a bridge teacher for about four years and a bridge director for 25 years. When she was active in duplicate from 1957 until she began directing around 1984, Mildred amassed over 7, 000 master points in the ABA. She is still listed in the top 100 ABA bridge players.

During all of this, Mildred had a career. She worked at the Office of the Secretary of Defense for 31 years. When she retired in 1979, she was Military Assistant Program Manager. She was the only African American in that position at that time. Mildred was happy to retire because she wanted to play bridge. Before she retired she would go to tournaments on the weekends, but she would be ready for work on Monday mornings. She did not neglect the job. Mildred says she loved her life in bridge. She attended all of the ABA national tournaments from 1958 until she became less active in the 1980s. She went to her first ABA national in 1958 without any points. When she left, she had won 25 master points. She would go to the national tournaments without a partner, pick one up, and win. She met Julius Fields from New York at a tournament in

Pittsburg, and they played together many years. She also played with John Jordan, III, for many years until she spent more time as a director. (John Jordan was one of the top ten ABA players before his illness and death.) Mildred remembers attending tournaments with WBU player Ted Austin and his wife. They went everywhere. She would pick up a partner to make the fourth for their team, and they were *very* successful. She recalls that even before Ted was an ABA life master, the team won the major and final team event of one national tournament. She says Ted treated them as if he were captain. He would tell them what to eat, and he would not let them eat much.

Mildred joined the ACBL in 1964, and she became an ACBL life master. She says she prefers the ABA to ACBL because of the friends she makes, like her best friend these days, Fannie (Boots) Smith. She says they have been friends for a long time, and even though they do not play tournament bridge anymore, they are still friends. Another best friend is Nora Tucker. They have been dear friends since 1957. She says in the ABA she gets a chance to talk and fraternize with the other players. She says she has played with many persons in ACBL, but none have really become close friends.

As to a merger between ABA and ACBL, Mildred says she prefers things just as they are. She thinks a merged bridge association would be too big. She remembers also when the ACBL did not want African Americans to join.

Nowadays, Mildred has retired to the Riderwood community in Maryland. They have bridge games at Riderwood every night, and Mildred plays every night. And she is still winning. She says her eyes are bad, she has glaucoma, sometimes she forgets what she is doing, but she still wins. She says they have bingo games at Riderwood, but she cannot play because she cannot see the card. Her friend Fannie marvels that she cannot see much and she forgets, but she does not forget her bridge.

There was a time that Mildred enjoyed directing bridge games as much as playing in them, but her preference now is playing. When the director of the bridge games at Riderwood was away for a month, Mildred's friends introduced her as a director and Mildred substituted for just that period. Mildred says she does not read books much anymore because of her glaucoma, but she still reads the newspaper everyday. She is an avid sports fan. She looks at all the basketball games. As a subscriber to the NBA cable network, she can see the games whether or not they are shown locally. She also likes football and tennis.

Mildred enjoys the Riderwood community. They provide excellent doctors and pharmacies that deliver medicine. Mildred tries to exercise and keep her weight under control. Because of back problems, she cannot walk or ride a bicycle. She exercises by rolling on the floor on an exercise wheel. Mildred gets around the Riderwood grounds on her automatic scooter. Riderwood has five restaurants where residents can eat dinner without paying. They must pay for breakfast and lunch at the restaurants if they choose not to cook in their own kitchens. Riderwood hires high school students to serve the residents in the dining room. The students must have A or B averages in school in order to work there. The residents are not allowed to tip the students, but they can contribute to the students' college funds. At the end of every year, Mildred contributes $1,000 to the scholarship fund of one student who has impressed her.

A product of racially segregated education, Mildred considers the practice ridiculous. She says it still exists today in some places. Residents of Riderwood are encouraged to make donations to the schools in the area. Mildred and her friends have refused to contribute to at least one school that has a reputation for mistreating black students. She enjoys television and radio ministry. In fact there is one minister she listens to every morning. She does not like gossip. She says if you gossip, people will gossip about you. She loves bridge. She says, "Whatever you do for bridge, I'm for it."

(Note: Mildred's interview was on December 13, 2007.)

Gladys Ashley

This story is about Gladys Ashley. She strikes you as a determined, hardworking person. That seems to be true about most of these senior members of the Washington Bridge Unit. They grew up making contributions to the betterment of the people and organizations with which they were involved, and they still make what contributions they can even now. Now Gladys is a North Carolinian by birth. She was born in Henderson, NC. Her birthday is February 22. Her father was a minister and a contractor in carpentry. As his ministry grew, he gave up contracting. Gladys had one sister and five brothers. Today only her sister and two of her brothers are still alive. She attended Concord grammar school in Franklin County and Albion Academy High School, which is in Franklinton City, NC.

Even though the schools were racially segregated, Gladys remembers no racial obstacles to getting an education. She has no particular preference when it comes to segregated versus integrated schools. Gladys loved it where she grew up in North Carolina. However, in 1941 Gladys' parents moved the family to Washington, DC.

Gladys met her husband in Washington at the home of one of his friends. Gladys and another friend had gone there to play cards, probably whist or pinochle. She and her husband were married in 1947. They divorced in the 1960s. They had two children—a son and a daughter. Their children both attended prestigious Catholic boarding schools in Richmond, Virginia. Tragically, her son was the victim of a street robbery in which he was struck in the head. Her son was in a coma for one month and never came out of it.

Today Gladys enjoys her daughter, granddaughter, and one great granddaughter. She sees them often, and she depends on her daughter for her weekly shopping. Gladys considers all of her friends best friends, but she has one friend locally with whom she runs around.

One of Gladys' main enjoyments is traveling. She takes regular vacations. She likes the North Carolina beaches, especially the Outer Banks. She once took a 33-day trip around the world. She says the most prejudice she experienced on that trip was boarding the bus that took them out of Washington. The only other time was on their return journey through England. During that trip she was in Japan during the World Fair there; and they were in Tel Aviv just a few days before the first airline hijacking. In addition to that trip she has traveled all over. She especially liked Mexico—all parts of it—and Canada.

Bridge is a longtime enjoyment of Gladys. She thinks it was in the early 1980s that she began playing bridge. She was on a trip to the slot machines in Atlantic City. An older bridge player asked Gladys to play her hand. Although the player was only dummy at the time, the exposure to the game piqued her interest.

Gladys had been doing pinochle at the Petworth Library in DC, and she decided to pursue bridge, not knowing how much was involved. The library had built extra rooms for meetings, etc. Gladys got a group together and asked a person to become their teacher in one of the rooms at the library. During the first year that the person taught, the members of the group would chip in to pay her as they saw fit. The second year the DC Recreation Department told the teacher she needed to be under contract. After the second year when there was no formal contract provided by the recreation department, the teacher decided to give up the class.

In 1985 Gladys took the ACBL class to become a certified bridge teacher. After passing the weeklong class, Gladys received certification. So, Gladys taught bridge at Petworth Library from 1985 through 1999. It was in 1999 that the Washington Bridge Unit purchased its bridge home. Then, Gladys taught at the WBU bridge home.

Gladys' most memorable bridge moment was winning a first place trophy at the WBU's 1986 Cherry Blossom Tournament. Her most memorable bridge partner was Cora Robinson. She and Cora played together from the time she began bridge until Cora moved to Chicago. Even then, they would meet from time to time to play in tournaments out of town. When Cora began walking with the aid of a cane, one of the bridge players, Herb Quarles, would tease Gladys that Cora had the cane to hit her over the head if she made a bad bid.

Gladys' favorite bridge locale is Las Vegas. She enjoyed attending the ABA western section's tournaments there. She liked the strong gathering of players there. In terms of preferences for one or the other of the two national bridge organizations—the ABA and the ACBL—Gladys thinks bridge is bridge whatever the organization. She thinks she has learned more from the ACBL since because of its large size, it can provide more classes.

Gladys' career was with the federal government where she worked for 35 years. She once turned in a suggestion that saved the government $250,000. She looked forward to her retirement, which was in 1978. The government gave her a retirement party. When Gladys retired, she bought a bent wood rocking chair. She jokingly told friends she would put everything in it except herself. And she meant it!

Gladys had her most prized accomplishments as a retiree. She volunteered for JACS (the Joint Action Community Service), which provided job corps jobs for those in need. In 1995 Gladys was the JACS National Volunteer of the Year. President Bill Clinton presented to her a silver-framed certificate signed by him. He did that at an award presentation on Capitol Hill. The DC government also gave her a certificate signed by Mayor Marion Barry. DC Congressional delegate Eleanor Holmes Norton gave a very nice, large party for her.

Religion is very, very important to Gladys. She was raised in a very religious home. She now belongs to the Divine Science Church in the Georgetown section of DC. Gladys' favorite books are sacred books; she reads the Bible everyday. Gladys enjoys her yearly family reunions.

Gladys has encountered racial obstacles on the job and in her volunteer work, but she overcame them. As to challenges, in general,

Gladys says there is one everyday. Her philosophy of life is: "To each his own; I don't judge you; you don't judge me." In reflection, Gladys says there is nothing she would do over.

(Note: Gladys' interview was on June 28, 2007.)

Nettie Banks

Nettie Banks is very pleased and happy to say she is 88 years old. She adds that 88 years is a good long time, but she hopes to live many more years. She was born June 6, 1919 in Birmingham, Alabama. However, she grew up in Greensboro, North Carolina, where her grandmother reared her. She loved growing up in Greensboro with her grandmother. She says her grandmother was a doll, and she would love to relive her life with her. Nettie had two brothers, one of whom lives today.

Nettie attended the Washington Street Elementary School and the James B. Dudley High School in Greensboro. After high school she attended Bennett College, where she received a BS degree, then on to Columbia University in New York where she earned an MA degree. Over the years Nettie has acquired more than 60 credits beyond the Master's degree. Nettie says there were no obstacles to her acquiring an education. Along with what she modestly calls a small scholarship after high school, her grandmother made college possible. She prefers integrated education although her schooling was in an all black environment until graduate school.

Nettie says she has always worked with little children, which she loves. Her career includes Director of Nursery Schools for Head Start, then Assistant to the Director followed by Director of Nursery Schools for her alma mater, Bennett College. Later Nettie became Director of Nursery Schools for North Carolina A&T College. It was there that she met her husband. When they met, he was a senior in electrical engineering. Later he taught mathematics at the college. In 1955 Nettie came to the Washington, DC area. She was expecting her third of four daughters. (Nettie's second daughter only lived twenty hours.) She came to be with her husband who had gotten a job at Hoffman Boston High School in Washington. Nettie's husband passed in 1966. Nettie was also Interim Principal at the Syphax Elementary School in Washington for one half school year, after which she went back to counseling. Her career continued until 1986 when she retired.

Nettie's three surviving daughters are Anita Dianne, Susan, and Carole. Like their parents the daughters are well educated. Nettie says they attended the schools of their choice. Dianne graduated from Dickenson College in Pennsylvania, and she has a Master's degree from the University of Wisconsin. Susan graduated from Emerson College in Boston, where she majored in mass communication. Carole graduated from Oglethorpe University in Atlanta, and she has an MS in international finance from George Washington University in Washington, DC. Dianne is now retired, but Susan and Carole hold down high-powered jobs with tremendous responsibility.

Like all the persons featured in this book, Nettie is a bridge enthusiast. She began playing social or party bridge when she was in college. It was not until she retired in 1986 that she began duplicate bridge. She joined the Washington Bridge Unit shortly after that. Nettie served as treasurer of the WBU in 1999 for a few years. She has enjoyed going to the WBU for tournaments as well as to out-of-town locales. Her favorite bridge locale is Las Vegas. She also likes Detroit where she reached the diamond level (about 2,000 master points). Other favorites are Atlanta and Chicago. Today Nettie plays regularly where she has her retirement condominium at the Riderwood Village. She also plays at the WBU on Tuesday mornings.

Nettie's memorable bridge personalities are her partners and fellow WBU members. Her best friend and long-term partner is Mary Gross. Others are Irene Thomas, Sam Dendy, Deloris Tolson, and Wilma Wood. Nettie stresses that she loves bridge, and because she is a people person, she enjoys the camaraderie. Of the two main national bridge groups, ABA and ACBL, Nettie prefers ABA. She recalls that ACBL did not permit African Americans to be members in the early days; so, she has played bridge mostly in the ABA. She would love to see a merger of the ABA and the ACBL, however. She thinks both organizations are growing smaller and a merger would be interesting.

Traveling has always been a major pastime for Nettie. Although she has traveled all over Europe, she has not been to Greece, but she would like to visit there. She has also traveled throughout Asia, including Hong Kong,

Singapore, and Thailand. In addition, she has enjoyed the Bahamas and California. Nettie's family has a reunion every two years, and she attends those. They are usually held in cities where family members live, such as Columbia, SC; Charlotte and Greensboro, NC; New York, and Baltimore. They usually stay in hotels. They have a reunion coming up in 2008. Nettie says she likes to be around people, and socializes a lot with the persons in her community. Nettie always enjoyed reading, but her eyes prevent her from doing that nowadays.

Nettie says if she were to do something over, it would be the fourth grade in elementary school, which she skipped. She thinks she may have missed some things. She is not in favor of school children skipping grades.

Religion has always been primary in Nettie's life. She is a longtime, active member of Fifteenth Street Presbyterian Church in Washington, where she is a deacon. She is also an associate member of Riderwood Village Church. She says she is less active in church now that she has become somewhat of an invalid.

The two persons Nettie admires most are affiliated with Fifteenth Street Church. They are Jacqueline Williams and former pastor, Reverend Doctor John L. Pharr. Nettie says she likes their intelligence, genuineness to the word of God, and how they express it.

Nettie's tips on longevity include God in the forefront of one's life. She says one must believe in God; know that he controls *everything* about us; know that he is a forgiving God, for he has forgiven her of many things. Additionally, she says we should do what we can to help others. She thinks many churches are in trouble these days. She thinks some religious leaders are so interested in money they have let the spiritual leadership suffer. She says she wants a religious leader who can get her to the Promised Land. She says, they say *they* are there but she wants them to help her get there.

Nettie says she just loves life!

(Note: Nettie's interview was on December 3, 2007.)

Josephine Caldwell

This story tells about Josephine Caldwell. Josephine is capable, industrious, and enterprising. She has a flexible mind. Josephine was born in New York City on October 9, 1923. She was the seventh of seven children. Today, she has two sisters and one brother still living. She attended New York City Public Schools, which were integrated. She graduated with honors from Washington Irving High School, receiving the highest score of any student, black or white, in the Geometry Regents. Mathematics was her favorite subject. She loved growing up in New York.

When she finished high school, Josephine received a scholarship to Howard University in Washington, DC. She attended Howard University and graduated magna cum laude— with high honors—in 1945. She received a BS degree in foods and nutrition. Howard University awarded her a graduate fellowship, which led to her MS degree in nutrition in 1947. It was at Howard University in 1941 that Josephine met her future husband, Elmo (Saint) Caldwell. In 1942 he enlisted in the US Army and served with distinction in Italy, receiving the Purple Heart. After his return they married in 1948.

Josephine and her husband had three daughters from their marriage. The first daughter is Paula Caldwell Drake, who lives in Ohio. Josephine currently lives in NW Washington, DC with her second daughter, Nkechi Taifa Caldwell Kearney. Her third daughter is Roberta Caldwell Kee, who has just relocated to Raleigh, NC. Josephine has eight grandchildren and five great grandchildren. She sees those who live locally all the time. The daughter and her family from Ohio visit on holidays, but they stay in touch otherwise. Josephine's family has reunions, not every year, but as often as possible. Josephine is now a widow. After 51 ½ years of marriage, her husband passed away in 2000. Josephine has many close friends, but she always thinks of her mother as her best friend. Even today, Josephine still follows her sage advice.

Josephine began her career as a chief dietitian at Providence Hospital in Baltimore, MD. She worked there for about three years. The rest of her career was in education. She first taught as an instructor in the Department of Home Economics at Howard University. After that she was a teacher, counselor, and administrator in the DC Public Schools. When she retired in 1985, she was assistant principal at Roosevelt High School in Washington, DC. She had been at Roosevelt since 1966, where she was a guidance counselor for two years and assistant principal the remaining years.

Of course, Josephine continued to prepare herself for her career while she worked. She attended New York University and Columbia University in New York City. She completed her requirements for counseling through DC Teachers College and George Washington University. She completed her requirements for supervision and administration in DC public schools at the University of Maryland and American University. While working, Josephine served as chair of the assistant principals' committee in the National Association of Secondary School Principals. She was also chair of the supervisory committee of the DC Teachers Federal Credit Union. Although she enjoyed her career, Josephine retired in 1985 because she had begun to experience health problems.

Josephine began playing bridge quite by accident, as she puts it. Back in 1995 or 1996, she was at the Fort Stevens Senior Center in NW Washington waiting to get a manicure. She wandered into a class, and she did not know what it was. It happened to be a bridge class. The teacher, WBU member Louis Griffin, invited her to come in. She went in, sat down, and was fascinated by the explanations and coverage. When she was leaving, the bridge instructor invited her back. She did exactly that, and that was her beginning in duplicate bridge. Josephine loved card games already. She played pinochle and bid whist. However, this was the first time she had formal instruction in a card game. She says she loved it. She enjoys the challenge of the game.

Since that class, Josephine has joined the WBU's Y-Bridgettes club. She has won trophies at the ABA national tournaments in 2000, 2002, and 2003. Her most memorable and thrilling achievement was winning the ABA Mid-Atlantic section's prestigious Calvin C. Rubens memorial trophy. For her category Josephine had won the most master points of any bridge player in the Mid-Atlantic section. Josephine says she loves all of the bridge teachers in the WBU, as well as her ACBL teacher.

Josephine's first bridge partner was WBU member Annie Moss. She also plays a lot with WBU member, Costella Tyler, with whom she played in the ACBL from time to time. She prefers the ABA to the ACBL, and she thinks a merger of the two organizations is not a good idea. Because the method of scoring games and awarding master points in the ABA is different from that in the ACBL, she thinks it would play havoc with longtime members of either organization. Josephine does not travel to bridge tournaments as often as she used to. Her favorite tournament locations include Atlanta, New Orleans, Las Vegas, and Jacksonville.

In addition to bridge, Josephine has many hobbies, and she is involved in many activities. She has done crafts, including macramé, whittling, and upholstery. She has made letter openers and animals. She likes to read, especially Shakespeare and the classics. She loves sports. This petite lady does, or has done, tennis, archery, judo, tai chi, and meditation. Her husband was a black belt judo instructor. He organized and taught a class in Kodokan judo at Albright Memorial United Methodist Church for over 30 years.

Josephine enjoys traveling, and she gets a trip in at least every year. She and her husband used to travel a lot. They visited most of the states in the US. Their travels include Greece, Rome, Paris, Switzerland, Hawaii, Alaska, the Caribbean, and Africa. The Point of No Return in Goree Island in Senegal affected her tremendously. It is the last stop in Africa Africans experienced before being shipped into slavery. Josephine's favorite vacation locale is Hawaii, where she has been twice.

Josephine's church is Albright Memorial United Methodist Church. She has always been very active in church work. She has served on the administrative board, the finance committee, and the board of the daycare center. Today, she is as active as she can be, given her health issues. Outside of church Josephine has been a member of a club called Fashionettes, Inc. for over 50 years. She has served them in most officer positions—president, vice president, secretary, and treasurer. Her husband was a member of the Omega Psi Phi black Greek fraternity. Josephine has been active with the Omega Wives, an offshoot of the fraternity.

Also an entrepreneur, for the past two years Josephine has owned an internet-based travel agency. She says it is both interesting and exciting. Consumers can visit her site, www.EquasiTravel.com and book their travel, day or night. The parent organization of the travel agency provides opportunities for fundraising for nonprofit organizations, which she plans to specialize in. In addition to these things, Josephine was the founder and first president of an investment club, C.H.I & Associates, the purpose of which was to expose its members to sound financial principles and investments.

In terms of obstacles in school and life, Josephine considers herself fortunate. She thinks college might not have been possible without her scholarships and fellowships. One incident stands out in her mind as possible racial prejudice. It was when she applied for a job at the US Department of Agriculture. Her college background was in research, and she sought a job in research. However, the USDA only offered her a job in their Beltsville, MD lab, which would consist primarily of feeding lab animals.

Josephine says she has experienced many physical challenges. For that reason she favors combining the holistic approach with traditional medicine. She is a graduate of the Hippocrates Health Institute in Boston and Florida. They recommend a vegetarian diet mostly made up of raw foods. They particularly recommend wheat grass in the diet. Josephine considers herself about 60 % vegetarian.

If Josephine were to do anything over, it would be to major in math in college. She says she did not take much math in college, but she has an affinity for it. She has many philosophies of life, but the basic one is the Golden Rule: Do unto others, as you would have them do unto you. One person she has admired most is Mary McLeod Bethune, an educator who was able to reach people very well. Josephine has enjoyed everything that she, herself, has done. She enjoys being with people. She says she loves people, and she particularly enjoys bridge people.

(Note: Josephine's interview was on May 16, 2008.)

Dr. and Mrs. Calhoun
(Cecelia and Noah)

This is the story of Cecelia and Noah Calhoun
who have been married for fifty-eight years.
Both are exceedingly accomplished and have
distinguished themselves highly in their fields
of endeavor and service to the community.
Noah's fields of service have been as oral
surgeon, professor, and researcher. He is
currently professor emeritus at Howard
University. He is as modest as he is
accomplished. Cecelia's field has been nursing,
education, and administration. She is elegant
and charming.

Cecelia was born in New Roads, Louisiana, which is about sixty miles from New Orleans. She says it is a small place similar to an island. The town is very Creole says Cecelia, and her background is Creole. It was also a very French town. Cecelia was born in the month of September. She grew up in Scotlandville, Louisiana. Because it is now part of Baton Rouge, you will not find it in an atlas. She grew up with her two sisters. She spent summers in New Roads, LA with her grandparents and other cousins. She recalls that her sweets back then were confined to the sugar cane her grandmother purchased twice yearly to share with all the grandchildren. Cecelia says she liked where she grew up, but because she is adaptable and non-territorial, she can enjoy almost any place. The Louisiana schools Cecelia attended were like the community. They included African Americans, Cajuns, and a few other groups. Her parents' strong emphasis on education had a great impact on her.

Noah was born in Clarendon, Arkansas on March 23, 1921. He grew up as an only child in St. Louis, Missouri. He says he liked growing up there, and he adds that when you are poor, you do not know about the rich. His grade and high schools in St. Louis were segregated. The schools were good; he learned Shakespeare with great joy.

Both Cecelia and Noah came to Washington, DC to attend school. It was there that they met. Noah says he has been in the DC area off and on since 1942. He came to attend dental school at Howard University School of Dentistry. Before he graduated from dental school in 1948 becoming a Doctor of Dental Surgery, Noah attended Fisk University in Nashville, Tennessee, Lincoln University in Jefferson City, Missouri, and the University of Pennsylvania in Philadelphia. Noah received hospital training at the old Freedman's Hospital in Washington, DC. His highest level of education is a Master of Dental Science, which he received from Tufts Medical and Dental School, studying there from 1953 to 1955. His extensive postgraduate training includes an impressive list of courses in oral surgery, oral pathology, oral trauma, and research methods.

After completing dental school and internship, Noah's professional career began in Tuskegee, Alabama where he was an oral surgeon at the

Veterans Administration (VA) hospital. His career has been highly distinguished. Some highlights of Noah's career follow. He was in charge of dental residents and intern training at the VA hospital in Tuskegee for several years. For several years he was a visiting professor at the Howard University School of Dentistry; he was also a professorial lecturer at the Georgetown University Dental College. Finally, he was chief of dental research at the Washington, DC VA hospital. As Cecelia says, Noah has been first in so many areas—in his field, in education, in training persons of all races in oral surgery.

Cecelia came to Washington, DC to follow an interest in going to medical school. At the time, she had already received a B.S. in liberal arts from Southern University in Louisiana. She did not have the money to send herself to medical school. Both her father and her church were very interested in her education. Her father was ill and died shortly after her arrival in Washington. Her church encouraged her to go to Catholic University and agreed to support her if she wanted to attend medical school. She did attend Catholic University, but she did not attend medical school. She received a B.S. in nursing education from the university. Cecelia says that although she was the first black female to live in residence in the health care area at Catholic University/Providence Hospital, she did not experience racial strife there. When she completed her nursing degree, Cecelia was offered a great job in administration. Although she now had two B.S. degrees, she did not consider herself qualified for the job. Having met Noah, she decided to take a job with the VA hospital in Tuskegee. It turned out to be a grand experience. It was in Tuskegee that Cecelia and Noah married in a small wedding ceremony in 1950. She says, somewhat jokingly, that if she did it over it would be a large, Hollywood style wedding.

When the couple returned to Washington, DC, Cecelia first worked for the VA hospital in Washington. Then, she won a scholarship to do graduate study at the University of Chicago. There, she earned an M.S. degree in nursing, education, and administration. She was the only African American female in her class there. Cecelia recalls that at the time the teachers at the university were politically savvy, and it was an exhilarating experience. It was during the time that Adlai Stevenson was running for president of the United States, and the students were kept aware by the politically astute professors.

Cecelia's experience at the University of Chicago was a first-hand exposure to the cultures of the world by living in the international house for students of different cultures. There, people talked and exchanged experiences. She thinks the experience helps her to understand and appreciate the credentials of US Senator Barack Obama, whom she supports in his efforts to become the first African American president of the United States. Also, when she was a student at the university, it had a president who was at the time the youngest president of a large university. Also contributing to the excitement of the times in Chicago was the mayor Richard Daley and thinkers like Mortimer Adler, the author of the Great Book. At the University of Chicago, Cecelia received and accepted an invitation to join the Pi Lambda Theta, University Women in Higher Education organization.

Cecelia's nursing career was long and distinguished. She retired from active nursing service in 1993, at which time she received many certificates of appreciation. Cecelia had a strong work ethic, and she did things to better her work environment and to encourage others to make the most of their jobs. She once told a chronic complainer, "Do a good day's work, then see what happens." She developed a new department, and she worked to help promote the department. She did not spend time with the persons who did not seek achievement. She received regular promotions, and she coached others on how to work for their promotions. She encouraged others to build their own self-esteem, rather than just saying, "He or she does not like me." She says be happy with all God has given you, and after doing all you can do, forget the whole thing. She has an illustrious list of improvements she made both in the work environment and for the nursing profession.

Cecelia and Noah have two children—a son, Stephen, who is a physician and a daughter, Cecelia, who is a dentist. The light of their lives is their granddaughter Kaira Cecelia Catherine who is a high school student in Washington, DC. One of Cecelia's enjoyable endeavors is serving as the family's archivist. She has prepared a collage depicting the life of her granddaughter from infancy to about age 6. It depicts her among persons who were important to her in those early years. She has also written about her granddaughter's development since the age of 7. Her granddaughter is now sweet 16 going on 17, and Cecelia is writing about her at age 15.

Cecelia says her family does not have regular family reunions because they are a relatively small family. They do get together with their family and the families of Cecelia's two sisters on holidays. Noah's best friend since dental school is Jeremiah Taylor. Although Cecelia has a number of close friends, she considers her daughter her very best friend. Her second best friend is one she made years ago in Tuskegee AL. Her name is Gloria Patterson. Cecelia says she and Gloria are both Catholic and they both have two children. They have kept in touch through the years, and they always greet each other with, "I love you."

Cecelia and Noah enjoy their lovely home in the Portals Estate section of NW Washington. Cecelia says she likes being at home. It contains an eclectic collection of the things she likes to share. They include the many results of her creative efforts. She has to go out to buy things or to see the doctor, but she likes being at home.

Like all the subjects in this book, the Calhouns play bridge, and they are current members of the WBU. They discovered that bridge was popular in Washington and that it was a good game for couples. They began bridge after taking an introductory course at the YWCA in the 1960s. Muriel and Charles Hanson, who are two of their favorite bridge personalities, introduced them to the WBU. Elizabeth (Bea) Woods is also a favorite of Cecelia. She says Bea has the perfect manners for bridge—she is very knowledgeable and very motivating. Noah's favorite partner is Conrad Hipkins, who is a member of the Bridgemasters WBU club. Noah has served as president of the Bridgemasters.

Cecelia and Noah also played social bridge with a group that included WBU members and the accomplished Doris Mitchell. The Calhouns also play bridge with the ACBL. They are voracious players together. Noah prefers the ACBL to the ABA because he thinks it is better organized with fewer disputes. He also thinks a merger between ABA and ACBL is a good idea. They have not taken bridge vacations.

The Calhouns' other hobbies include chess, canasta, reading, checkers, ballroom dancing, and traveling, especially cruises. They say they used to have house parties, but now they do small entertaining with four to six guests. Noah especially enjoys reading poetry. Recently, a book by Lee Strobel called *The Case for Jesus Christ* has fascinated him. The author uses his legal secretarial background and the rules of evidence to analyze Christ as documented in the four gospels and by other authors. Cecelia says reading is a favorite pastime for her. Her favorite authors include John Adams, Jane Austen, and Mark Twain. *Invictus* is her favorite poem. Another favorite poem is *The House by the Side of the Road*, which was a favorite of her oldest sister. She says *The Cultural History of the US* and *The Cultural History of the World* keep her grounded.

The couple's travels have taken them far and wide. They have been all over the world—to Europe, Asia, and Africa. They say their deep African travel was limited to Tanzania. Their signature vacation is Martha's Vineyard. It was their first vacation together, and they try to return there periodically. They have a large plaque on the wall in their kitchen with decals from the many countries they have visited. Cecelia says Noah likes to visit different places. They like to see how the rest of the world lives—not just where to buy souvenirs or to sit on the beach. On a visit to Spain they went to a restaurant that took patrons into the kitchen. In Majorca guests shared tables with celebrities. Cecelia particularly likes to see the museum, the zoo, and a good restaurant when she visits a country. She thinks those tell a lot about the people who live there.

Cecelia was born a Catholic in predominately Catholic Louisiana. Noah converted to Catholicism when they married. Cecelia says growing up, the Catholics were not allowed to visit or connect with non-Catholics. She is Catholic to the core. However, as an adult she has learned about other religions and respects them.

The Calhouns are members of St. Michael's Catholic Church in Silver Spring, MD, where Cecelia serves as a lector and is a member of the Sodality. Cecelia enjoys Catholic music especially "Ave Maria," "the Gregorian Chant," and "Come Holy Ghost." Cecelia was very moved by their trip to Jerusalem. There they saw the table where Jesus sat with the 12 Apostles. They also saw, among other things, where Jesus walked on water. She says it was both inspiring and amazing. So much is written about Jerusalem in the bible, and it is such a small place.

In addition to church work, both Calhouns are members of numerous professional, social, and service organizations. For example, Noah is a member of the Institute of Medicine, National Academy of Science. He is also a member of the first black Greek organization, the Alpha Phi Alphas. Cecelia includes among her organizations the first black female Greek organization, the Alpha Kappa Alphas. She is also a member of Jack and Jill of America and the Links. They always give back to the community, support charitable organizations, and do volunteer work. They want to help make the world a better place.

With respect to obstacles and challenges in life, Noah says it was quite a struggle in early dentistry. They tried to keep blacks out of the

American Oral Surgery Society. He says they had to fight to get in and to even be examined for accreditation as oral surgeons.

In articulating his philosophy of life Noah says:

> As I look at life and I look at the animals, I think we were put here for reproduction. And I go along with Jesus: Love thy God with all thy heart and might and treat thy fellow man as thyself.

If he were to do anything over it would be to be as much in social issues as in science. He thinks he was too much on the practical side and being in politics or government might have been interesting. He admires Nelson Mandela, Bishop Desmond Tutu, and his family—son, Stephen Marc; daughter, Cecelia Noel; his granddaughter, Kaira Cecelia Catherine; and wife Cecelia Jane Christopher Calhoun.

Cecelia's philosophy of life is broad. She says we are all created for more than we can possibly realize. You have to go forward; you can't keep going back and saying, "look what I did." What are you doing today? Even if you have a deficiency, you keep trying to move forward. She also says:

> I like to feel that I've made a difference—to the family, to the community, and then to reach out to the world. I'm the type of person who thinks your thoughts are just as important as your actions. They indicate what is going on inside a person. If you do not have the right thoughts, people can read through that. I just believe in fairness and goodness and we can always remember there is a merciful God; if not, we might as well give up.

She thinks some of that is missing from human behavior now.

Cecelia further states:

> I find as I grow older, I like to be more patient and avoid worry. Just do what you can about it. I try to do that. That takes great effort too. I find one way to do that is to be more grateful for what you have.

Finally she says:

I really feel we have a responsibility to do whatever we do to the best of our ability. I don't mean we can do all. But whatever it is--cooking, cleaning, when greeting someone--do we do it from the heart?

There are things that Cecelia would like to continue more so than do over. She would like to visit more of the world to see how different things are in different parts of the world. She would also like to write more about her family. She admires Martin Luther King, Jr., especially because he was so young when he led the civil rights movement in this country.

(Note: The Calhouns' interview was on February 17, 2008.)

Iris Carr Story

A first impression of Mrs. Iris Carr is a lady of grace and beauty. It is later that you learn how spunky she is. She was born in a little town in Texas called Cox's Providence. That was on June 16, 1913. Iris did not remain in Cox's Providence long because the family moved to Taylor, Texas. She went to school in Taylor, and she graduated from high school there when she was 13 years old. At the age of 14, Iris entered Prairie View College. She graduated from college when she was 18 years old. She began teaching almost immediately in Wharton, Texas.

Iris worked while she was in college. Her parents were educators, but they did not have the money to put the children through college. Both Iris and her brother were in college at the same time. When her sister came to Prairie View during Iris' senior year, she got a second job at the college. In that way she was able to help her brother and sister with their expenses.

Iris says she has worked since she was nine years old and she has driven a car since that same age. The summer when she was nine years old, her father was in Pullman service. That summer her mother had taken her brother to the Mayo Clinic to see why he did not grow—he was a midget. The rest of the family stayed with her father's sister in Cleburne Texas, which was his birthplace. Her father had to meet the train for his job in Ft. Worth. Nine-year-old Iris would drive the car the 30 miles to Ft. Worth so that her father could meet his train. She drove the same distance back to Cleburne, of course. When it was time, she would drive back to Ft. Worth to bring her father home. As you can imagine, other drivers were very surprised to see the nine-year old behind the wheel. She remembers that very well. No one else in the family had a car, so it was her duty to drive her father. She did not need a permit to drive. In fact, she did not get a permit until she moved to Washington, DC years later. Iris adds that she drives even now, and on the freeway.

In general, Iris attended racially segregated schools, and she thinks that was just fine. In fact, in those days before desegregation, you could not find a better college than Prairie View. The problem was that the highest degree a person of color could get in Texas was a Bachelor's degree. They would not allow African Americans to attend Texas University. So, during the summer she would attend Columbia University in New York.

Most of the teachers went somewhere in the summer to get higher education. It was during those summers at Columbia that Iris fell in love with New York City. She recalls how safe it was to ride the subway alone. She was not afraid to go anywhere anytime, day or night. She would even drive from Texas to New York to go to school. In later years, Iris completed coursework for a Master's degree at Howard University. She lacked the dissertation for the degree. She had begun work on a dissertation on rural education in Texas, but because of job responsibilities, she was unable to complete it.

Iris taught in Texas for 12 years, and at a point she became very concerned about her future. As she puts it, back in 1943, they would not allow teachers of her descent to pay into teachers' retirement. She took a Civil Service examination for a job in Washington, DC so she could have something to look forward to in retirement. In addition, African American teachers received very low salaries. So, when she got a job with the federal government in Washington, she was getting twice as much money for half as much work. Iris remained in Washington 53 years. She left Washington for Dallas to be with her sister when her sister became disabled. Her sister had taught in Dallas for 43 years.

Iris began playing bridge when she was teaching in Austin, Texas. There were several teachers who wanted to play, so they formed a club and learned a little about bridge. It was at her job at the Recorder of Deeds in Washington in 1944 that the man who was to become her husband introduced Iris to the world of tournament duplicate bridge. That man was one of the lawyers who had regular business at the Recorder of Deeds. One day, he invited her to play in a tournament bridge game. She was reluctant at first because she could not anticipate how it would be. However, after the first game she decided she liked it. She says the difference between contract bridge and duplicate bridge was you could win without holding all the good cards. Defense is important in duplicate, and you can win more games on defense than playing the hands. So, in 1944 she joined a duplicate group.

Iris' first national ABA tournament was in 1947 in Atlantic City. (She recalls that Dr. Belsaw was president of the ABA at the time.) She and the lawyer had formed a partnership. He had accumulated some master points, but Iris had none. So because she had no points, she was not allowed to play with a master, which he was. In order for them to play together at the tournament, she had to very quickly earn at least 10 master points. She could enter the women's pairs if she could find a partner. She found a lady from New Orleans named Cherry Perryman. Iris offered to pay the entry fee for both of them if she would play with her in the women's pairs. They played together, and at

the half Ms. Perryman told Iris they were
having a good game. So, she gave Iris back her
money. At the end of the game, Iris and her
partner had won the women's pairs. She got the
10 points she needed, and from then on she
could play with her partner Dewey Carr (the
lawyer). Iris noted that you get 40 or 50 master
points for winning the women's pairs today.

Iris later married her bridge partner, Dewey
Carr. They were loyal and stalwart WBU
members from the beginning. When she joined
WBU, there were not many female members.
The men outnumbered the women two to one.
There were only three tables of women, not
even enough to have a women's pairs game. It
started that the men would go to the bridge club
every Friday night, leaving the women alone.
The men were in the Bridgemasters WBU club.
So a group of women who were the wives and
girlfriends of the Bridgemasters organized a
women's club. One of the women, a
mathematician named Ethel Grubb, gave the
group the name Dubridgettes.

Iris played regularly with Mary Russell, the
wife of a Dr. Russell. They were partners for a
long time, and they fared pretty well; in fact,

they had a very good partnership. Both their
husbands belonged to the Bridgemasters.
Another long-term bridge partner was Ella Mae
House whose sister was Iris' dearest friend in
college. Iris and Ella Mae were partners until
Ella Mae died. Their husbands were fraternity
brothers.

Later, the Duos club was born. It was a
husband and wife club that met on Sundays.
The Duos were reluctant to invite the Carrs to
join their club because they had so many master
points. Most of them had come into bridge
after the Carrs. Later on, however, the Duos
invited them to join. Iris still belongs to both
the Dubridgettes and the Duos. In fact, since
moving back to Texas, Iris comes back annually
to the WBU, and she hosts a party for the clubs.
Her late husband has been vice president of the
ABA. In fact, Dewey Carr was a charter
member of the ABA when it was formed at
Buckroe Beach, VA. Both he and Iris have
been honored with life membership in the ABA.

One of Iris' most memorable bridge moments
involved playing on a team of four women at an
Atlanta tournament. Iris' team was the lowest
ranking team. In ABA knockout games, the

lowest ranking team always plays the highest-ranking team in the first round. The loser is knocked out of the competition. The top ranking team was made up of Roscoe Alexander, Leon Jones, Caesar Baron, Joe Henry, and Oliver Cassell. The team was so confident of beating the ladies that they allowed the weakest four to play them. Well, Iris's team defeated the top ranking team and knocked them out of the competition. Iris' team was very excited, but they were knocked out in the second round.

Iris has had many favorite bridge personalities over the years, but two couples stand out for her. One was Sonny Hawkins and his wife. They seemed to own the mixed pairs. The other couple was Doris and Byron Brooks. Notwithstanding their status, they were very cordial and congenial. They were also helpful, and they did not mind new players, which Iris was at the time.

Iris has not played extensively in the ACBL, mainly because they did not permit African Americans in their games in the early years. She does remember that she was player of the year the first year they were allowed in ACBL games. She prefers the ABA because she likes the safety and honesty that prevails throughout the membership and the loyalty of "bridge friends." Once at an ABA tournament, a man lost his wallet containing $500, and when he got it back, the $500 was intact. She thinks it has been very difficult to lose anything of value in the ABA world.

We noted earlier that Iris' career has included teaching and government service. After leaving teaching in Texas, Iris worked at the Recorder of Deeds. At the same time she taught mathematics at the evening school for electricians. While working at the evening school, Iris met a lady who worked for the National Security Agency (NSA). Iris was disillusioned with her job at the Recorder's office because of what she considered sexual harassment. The lady from NSA offered to take Iris' résumé to NSA, where they hired her as a cryptologist. She later became a personnel officer. She worked for NSA for 23 years. In 1971 Iris retired early because of her husband's failing health.

Iris calls herself a religious fanatic, because religion is at the top of her list. She has always gone to church and worked diligently there. She was a member of the 19th Street Baptist Church in Washington, DC, and she joined the Helping Hand club there—and help is what they did.

Iris says, unfortunately, she has not had children of her own because she cared about children very much. When she taught, she always liked the children, and she met their parents. They all got along fine.

When Iris worked, she always saved her vacation leave so that she could attend the bridge tournaments. Her favorite bridge locale is New York City because there is so much to enjoy there, such as the theater. One special non-bridge vacation was a tour of Europe she did with her husband. They took a plane into London, then a boat across the North Sea to the Hook of Holland, then a bus tour of Holland and six other European countries. After Iris lost her husband, she enjoyed taking cruises with her sister. They took cruises to Alaska and Mexico. Even though she had been to Mexico twice before, it was her first time there on a cruise. She enjoyed a two-week vacation in Hawaii, and she would like to go back there.

Iris was very close to her sister. (Her sister passed this year—2007.) ABA players remember fondly the sight of Iris and her sister dressed identically at all the national tournaments.

Iris continues to enjoy bridge, and at the 2007 ABA Summer National, Iris' name was listed as winner of some events. Besides bridge, the only hobby Iris finds time for is reading. She cannot remember the authors' names, but there is one author whose every book she has read. His stories were true to life, and one book was called *Mixed Blessings*. It was about people who were in mixed marriages, and the stories were based on true-life situations.

Her best friends have been her roommate when she began teaching in Austin, Texas--Effie Bowls from Victoria, Texas--and a midget who worked with her at the Recorder of Deeds. She says Effie really knew how to be a friend. The coworker from the Recorder of Deeds was her best friend while she lived in Washington. Iris was the executor of her estate when she died. Iris' family has regular reunions, but she has not attended one since she left Washington, DC.

The reunions were usually in Alabama where her mother's family originated.

With respect to challenges, Iris says getting up every morning has been a challenge. But her greatest challenge over the years has been fending off men who have tried to compromise her. Sometimes, the offenders were even friends of her father. In addition, Iris started work very early, sometimes working in the households of others. Often the man of the house would try to compromise her. She reacted by, right then and there, calling the offender's wife to let her know what was happening. She even once poured the hot coffee she was serving on one offender.

Iris' philosophy of life is: do all the good you can for everybody that you can all the times that you can; and try to help somebody everyday. Iris says there are some things she would do over, in terms of avoiding some things. She says when she was a little girl she asked her father, a Baptist minister and principal of the high school, "How can we tell if we love God." Her daddy told her a cute poem in reply:

> Abu Ben Adam made his tribe increase.
> He awoke one night from a deep dream of peace

And he saw within the moonlight in his room
Making it rich like a lily in bloom
An angel writing in a book of gold
Exceeding peace made Ben Adam bold
And he said, what writeth thou?
The angel said, I'm writing the names of those
that love the Lord
Is mine one? said Abu.
Nay, not so replied the angel
He said I pray thee then write mine as one that
loves his fellow man
The angel wrote and vanished
And the next night he came
To read the names of those the love of God had
blessed
And lo, Ben Adam's name led all the rest.

Iris concludes:

According to the Bible: Whatever you do
to the least of them, you do to me. So I
knew what I had to do: Look for good in
everyone. Then you'll like everyone. I
do not like to see people abused. The
Passion of the Christ was so disturbing.
How could God let that happen to his own
son! How could people do that!

(Notes: Iris' interview was on July 31, 2007.
She passed away on April 26, 2008.)

John Coleman

This is the story of John Coleman. He has worked hard at building up the educational program for bridge players at the Washington Bridge Unit. John Coleman was born in Knoxville Tennessee on August 3, 1919. Because his father was a railroad fireman and did not have enough seniority to gain a fulltime position in Knoxville, the family moved to Chattanooga. They were in Chattanooga from about 1921 to 1932. It was in Chattanooga that John attended elementary and junior high school. When the family moved back to Knoxville in 1932, John was ready for high school. John graduated third in his class from Austin High School in 1936. He attended Knoxville College for a while.

Compared to the treatment of people of color in the rest of the south, John considered growing up in Knoxville favorable in many ways. People of color did not have to move off the sidewalk when a white person passed by. Early on, the town had three black mail carriers and two black police officers. What was interesting was that the black policemen could not arrest white persons. They would call for a white policeman and hold the persons until the white policeman came to arrest them. After World War II two of John's brothers became firemen in Knoxville. His youngest brother even became fire marshal in the 1950s.

In 1939 John left home for the first time to work for the Tennessee Valley Authority, which covered southern states. He worked on the Gilbertsville project in southwest Kentucky. John was 20 years old at the time. In fact, he was the baby of his work group. He worked two years in that particular setting. An interesting aspect of the setting was a place called Grandma River. The men went over the Grandma River to gamble. John did not participate in that. However, one of the men was an inveterate gambler, and he would gamble on anything. That man loved to play bridge, and he needed a bridge partner. At the time it was auction bridge, and the men played for 1/10 penny per point. (Some bridge scores could add up to thousands of points.) Not only did John not know how to play bridge, but also the possible losses were more than he could afford. The inveterate gambler offered to teach John bridge and to cover any losses. In addition, he would give John his share of the winnings. John thought it was a no-brainer to play with the man given the incentives. Since John did play bid whist, the man taught him the transformation from bid whist to bridge. John played with the man for the two years that he was on the job. After that John left bridge for a while.

John served in the military during World War II. He left the service in December 1945. He came to Washington, DC in 1946, with the intention of going to Howard University to become a doctor. He thought it would be easier to get into medical school at Howard University if he had an undergraduate degree from the school; so he enrolled in undergraduate school there.   However, the following year, John's father slipped on a front step and broke his back. He was confined to crutches for the rest of his life. So, John gave up his medical school plans. As the oldest in the family he had to help support the family financially.

It was not until coming out of the service that John really became hooked on contract bridge. The person most responsible for his getting into contract duplicate bridge was Sam Etheridge. Sam had been on the bridge circuit for several years. Sam and John were very close, and many persons thought they were brothers when they were both at Howard University. John had no formal lessons in bridge until 1952-53 when the bridge expert Fred Karpin had a class at the Van Ness center in Washington, DC. It was there that John met the person who was to become his long-term bridge partner—Mary Coleman. (Having a regular bridge partner is not as important to bridge players as having a life mate, but it is still very important.)

John met the love of his life, Gert, in 1949. He was a boastful, proud suitor. When he first saw Gert, he thought she was the prettiest thing he had ever seen. It was on the campus of Howard University that they met. John remembers thinking, "That's for me!" He was just a little discouraged when he used to see her around campus with a young man who he assumed was a suitor. It turned out the young man was her brother. John found out in recent years that the brother was actually his advocate. Their first real date was at the Mardi Gras ball given by the Omega Psi Phi fraternity. That was in March, which was close to Gert's birthday on March 19. Things went well because John gave her his fraternity pin in June. The pin was like an engagement ring.

John and Gert were married in August 1950. Their marriage lasted until Gert passed away after 56 short years. Gert was the center of John's world for all those years. She was his best friend. He thinks they were truly blessed because they thoroughly enjoyed each other. He remembers the early days when they would sit on the couch and the sun would start shining through; they would have sat up all night talking and laughing. John's Gert was born in

1915, and she died in 2006. They were blessed with a son and a daughter, four grandchildren, and two great grandchildren. John sees his family regularly.

Religion is very important in John's life. It was Gert who got him back on track with religion. When he met Gert, he had been out of the church for almost 20 years. She told him she wanted to raise their children in a church setting, and she asked him to please consider going back to church. He told her he would do that as soon as he found one that suited him. He wound up going to All Souls Unitarian Church for almost 35 years. (That church was very active in the civil rights movement of the 1960s.) John taught the Bible for three years, and he taught the major religions of the world to eighth graders for eight years. John is now a member of People's Congregational United Church of Christ.

Bridge was a major element in both John and Gert's lives. Gert also played bridge. They would travel to all the major ABA tournaments to play with their partners. One of John's favorite bridge locales was Atlanta, Georgia. John has played bridge in the ACBL as well as the ABA. He thinks it is important to have both exposures in bridge. In fact, in addition to his high ranking as a bridge player in the ABA, he is a life master in the ACBL. He is not certain the merging of the two bridge organizations would be a good thing. He would not want the ABA to lose its identity and its leaders in the process. John recalls that until about the mid 1960s people of color were not permitted to play in ACBL sanctioned games. They were not permitted to buy entries. He remembers clearly that they were turned away when they tried to buy entries. As a matter of fact the only place people of color could play in sanctioned ACBL games was at the Woodner Hotel on 16th Street, the State Department basement, and the Health, Education, and Welfare (HEW) building after hours.

John and Gert both loved dancing. Gert was quite the dancer. It was a treat to see them on the dance floor. John has also been a jazz enthusiast since the early 1930s. Today he has an extensive collection of long playing jazz albums. Album covers even decorate the walls of his den. John's favorite book is *On Being a Real Person* by Harry Emerson Fosdick. That book was a Christmas gift one year from his high school English teacher. He also enjoys a pamphlet by Josiah Ross called *Choice*.

After WWII John graduated from Howard University in 1948 with a degree in Economics. It was virtually unheard of at the time for a black person to get a job as an economist. The exception was if he had a Ph.D., he could teach in a black college or university. It turned out that if an economics major had at least 9 credits in statistics there was less of a problem getting a job. John had 12 credits in statistics by the time he finished his Master's degree at American University. He believes he may have been the first black graduate research assistant in statistics at American University.

The practice with many black college graduates at that time was to start out in the federal government in a clerical position planning to work up to a position in their fields. John's first mentor in graduate school advised him against doing that. He said if John began in a clerical position, he would probably never move out of that job category. He advised John to start his career with a private research firm. Then he would have a better chance of advancing in the federal government. John joined and worked in a private research firm for about 1½ years before he transferred to the federal government.

John loved statistics. His last position was chief of the statistical methods division at the Bureau of Labor Statistics. He thoroughly enjoyed his career. He retired in 1979 toward the end of the Carter administration. When his boss had retired, he was offered the opportunity to be groomed for that position. That would have been as a member of the Senior Executive Service (SES), where one served at the pleasure of the President. John refused that. He was already at the top of the government pay scale, and he already had the only job in which he was interested. John received many awards and commendations for his government service.

John almost died of a heart attack in 1969. He offloaded responsibilities at that time. That included giving up the Ph.D. program he had just begun to pursue. John's philosophy of life is: There is a destiny that shapes our end; we are responsible for most of what happens to us. If he were to do anything over, it would be to remedy the mistakes of the first 20 to 25 years of his life.

John's Gert 1950s

(Note: John's interview was on May 16, 2007)

Mary Gross, Ed.D.

A few years ago a bridge partner and I chatted with Mary Gross at the bridge table, and she told us she was 80 years old. I was floored. Not only is she a strikingly pretty person, but she looks at least 30 years younger. Mary is now 86 years old. She was born September 16, 1921 in Washington, DC, and that is where she grew up. Mary says she loved her life and growing up in DC. Things were racially segregated, but the black community provided everything for itself. Mary was born on Champlain Street in the Adams Morgan section of Washington. When she was three years old her family moved to

Florida Avenue just below North Capitol Street. That is the neighborhood where she grew up.

Mary recalls a vibrant black culture, and she *loved* it. She remembers how they could walk all over the city. There were concerts and museums, and her father would take her and her brothers and sisters to the circus when it would come to the market on 5th Street. They could walk to Union Station and the Library of Congress. It was a wonderful life. Mary was one of nine siblings, and seven of them are alive today—all in their seventies and eighties. They were all 2 or 2 ½ years apart. Two of Mary's siblings have been involved in the bridge scene. A brother, Jim Janifer, and his wife Libby continue to play today. Mary says he loves to play. Her sister, Rachael Guy, once played but no longer plays.

Mary attended DC Public Schools. Elementary school was John F. Cooke School. Junior high was at Terrell Jr. High, and high school was Dunbar High School. She graduated from Miner Teachers College in Washington. Later, Mary got a Masters degree from New York University (NYU) School of Education, followed by an Ed.D. from Nova Southeastern

University in Fort Lauderdale Florida. So, she is Dr. Mary Gross.

Mary remembers no obstacle to her getting an education. Even though she was poor, her undergraduate education was so inexpensive that she would manage to get the money. Then, in graduate school she had income of her own. She emphasizes there were no obstacles, just the *will* to get it. Race was not an obstacle. Mary's first white teacher was at NYU.

Mary met her husband while a graduate student at NYU. He was from Philadelphia Pennsylvania. They were married 52 ½ years when he died. They had three children—two daughters and one son. Her children live in the suburbs of Washington—the son in Bethesda Maryland, one daughter in Fairfax, VA, and the other in Hyattsville, MD. Mary has five grandchildren and five great grandchildren. A 6th is on the way. The grandchildren and great grandchildren are scattered, and Mary spends lots of time traveling to visit them. She says as a family they pushed their kids to finish college. They all did. Now, they are pushing the grandkids, and so far they are reaching the goal. Mary adds that her son is very much younger than her daughters. He was born when Mary was 42 years old. The daughters' children are all grown.

Mary had strong feelings about segregated versus integrated school settings for her children. She sent her children to historically black colleges, and she has not regretted it. She wanted them to have experiences with blacks that would help them know from whence they came. Her son's high school experience at racially integrated St. John's College High School was also a factor. She and her husband felt their son had missed some of the black experience. When their son was considering colleges to attend, his high school counselors knew nothing about the historically black colleges and universities. They steered him to predominantly white colleges. Their son went to North Carolina State for one year, and he hated it. At that point Mary and her husband took charge and sent him to Howard University. He did beautifully there. Mary's daughters went to Hampton University, where they were very happy. Mary's grandchildren went to Morgan State University in Baltimore, and she says they were so happy there. They all met their spouses there.

Mary's career was completely in education in the DC Public Schools. When she retired in 1976, she was Supervisor of Special Education for DC Public Schools. Starting in the 1940s, Mary was a teacher for several years. Next followed the job she loved most—guidance counselor in the elementary schools. She was a counselor for five or six years before she became supervisor of special education. Because the schools were beginning to change, she was happy to retire when she did. Mary's husband was in charge of adult education for the DC Public Schools, so after retirement she helped by working part time for eight years in adult education.

Mary taught primarily in Washington's racially segregated school system. Even after the 1954 Supreme Court decree mandating racially integrated schools, there was just a trickle of white students; but mainly they fled to the suburbs. For 20 or so years she taught in the Deanwood and Kenilworth sections of NE Washington. After that she taught in NW, near Cleveland Elementary School and the Howard Theater. When she became a counselor, she moved to LaSalle School, which is near Riggs

Road in NE Washington. Before her final
assignment as Supervisor of Special Education,
Mary became a supervising teacher at DC
Teachers College.

Religion is very high on Mary's list. She is an
ordained elder at Northeastern Presbyterian
Church. She says she has attended church
since childhood, and she is pretty well grounded
in religion. She has not always been
Presbyterian. As a child her parents took her to
a Methodist church, but they were so busy
rearing their nine children that Mary took
church in her own hands. While she was in
elementary school, a friend took her to her
church—Israel Colored Methodist Episcopal
(CME) Church. Mary's brothers and sisters
followed her to that church; so that became
their home church. Mary's husband joined the
Presbyterian Church after they were married, so
Mary changed with him.

Mary loves to travel. It is one of her favorite
things to do, and she has traveled throughout
the world. She loves Europe, Asia, and the
Caribbean Islands. She did a lot of traveling
with her husband and also with groups. She
travels nowadays with her friend, WBU

member Lillian Howard, who also loves to travel. Her son also loves to travel. He took her to Costa Rica. Whenever someone says let's go, she is ready. Mary says there is a lot to see and learn in this world. She enjoys the exercise room and the dancing that her retirement condominium community provides. (In fact, many of the persons written about in this book have retired there.)

Mary also enjoys her family. She is working on compiling a family history. She has accumulated and written down all the history from her family. She wants to leave the history as a legacy to her children. She says her family has attempted to have reunions, but few have materialized since her mother's passing. She thinks southern families are more likely to have reunions than city families. However, her family often reserves a park and brings all the children for a gathering for a day. Mary likes to read. Currently she is reading US Congressman Charles Rangel's book. She likes to keep up with the politicians to see what they are thinking. To a comment that US Senator Barack Obama should not give up in his quest to become US president, Mary says "give up" is not part of her vocabulary.

Of course, Mary enjoys bridge. She began playing socially after she retired in 1976. She used her knowledge of whist, and she says they really played a game of luck and guessing. Her partner had a little knowledge of the game, and he tried to teach the others. They played in the neighborhood of Northeastern Presbyterian Church. After doing that for several years, someone told her there would be duplicate bridge at Northeastern. So, her group went there and began to play. They had a difficult time because they were untrained. Somewhere along the line, Mary's very best friend, Nettie Banks retired, and Mary asked her to be her partner. Nettie agreed to do that. Up until then, Mary had no regular partner. She and Nettie began to study together and to travel to the tournaments. They were lower ranking players at that time, and they played in the sections designated for lower ranking players. They had a wonderful time. They had basic bridge classes, and various teachers came in.

Eventually, the duplicate bridge group at Northeastern became the Y-Bridgettes because they had met at the YWCA. Rita Davenport, a fellow player, had interceded at the church, and the church let them have a bridge home there. The Y-Bridgettes were the largest group in the WBU. They played every Wednesday. Even though their membership has fallen, they are still today WBU's largest club, and they still have their weekly game on Wednesdays. Mary says they had a glorious time. Mary's favorite bridge locale is Las Vegas.

In tournament duplicate bridge players earn points (master points) and move up through the ranks. With the help of more advanced bridge players who encouraged her, Mary easily earned points to reach the Ruby level of play. Memorable bridge moments include going to an ABA National and winning a clock in knockout teams and winning a pair event at another National. In the pair event that she won, Mary played with a partner whom she had just met. She says she was just overwhelmed at that success.

Mary's favorite bridge personalities are higher ranking players who have practiced with her. She acknowledges Ted Austin, in particular. He and his wife Marcea used to come to Mary's home in the early years, and they would teach Mary and her husband. Then, when she became better at bridge, she took lessons from Elizabeth Woods. Rose Ann Elliot would play with her even though she had many, many points. Mary also took lessons from Lou Garner. Others who mentored her were Faye Burke, Jerrie Thomas, Clarice Reid, and John Coleman.

Mary has achieved the diamond level (acquiring about 2,000 master points). She feels stuck there. Since then, she says she has had difficulty competing, mainly because of not keeping pace with the latest bridge conventions and trends. She says that since she has been at her Riderwood community (in suburban Maryland), she has had the great fortune of studying with John Coleman. In that way she is catching up with a lot of bridge conventions that she missed. Many bridge players, both ABA and ACBL, have retired to Riderwood, and there is a bridge game almost every night. The Riderwood games are not for master points, but some of the players compete for money.

As to preferences between ABA and ACBL, Mary prefers ABA. She says she has invested so many years of her life in ABA bridge. She also attributes that preference to the inability to

play in ACBL in the early days. She considers
some of the virtues of ACBL to be very good
teachers and classes and efficiently run games.
Mary would regret the demise of the ABA, but
due to its declining membership, she thinks it
might merge with ACBL in the distant future.

Mary says she has had many challenges in life.
She recalls fending for herself after her
husband's death as one. After his passing she
had to make a decision about where to live.
Her children wanted her to live with them, but
she preferred to be on her own. At first, she
purchased a condominium in Silver Spring,
MD, but she did not like that. Eventually she
chose Riderwood. When someone ran into her
car, Mary had to deal with insurance
companies, collision companies, etc., on her
own. Mary says the other challenge is trying to
stay healthy. She has had health issues, such as
implanted lenses from cataract surgery. She has
a problem with her voice, which she feels limits
her participation. She gets treatments for her
voice problem.

Mary cites the reaction to her as a special
education professional as a past obstacle. She
says for special education, Washington was

divided into divisions. Mary's division was the predominantly white area west of Rock Creek Park. When she would go there for special education matters, the schools would not admit to her that they had special education students. Mary knew that each school had at least one special education student, who often was relegated to areas such as the school basement. The schools did not want to acknowledge Mary's authority. That would happen often, but she managed to get her message across.

A person Mary has admired most is a past minister at Northeastern, Reverend Shelton B. Waters. She relates:

> He came there when the church was first integrated; and he did a tremendous job in pulling that church together. He is now in retirement. He is just a wonderful person. He worked pulling two races together. I have never seen anybody who could do it so effectively. The situation was the current church, which was located at 22nd and Varnum, was basically a dying church, and the minister there was white, and the parishioners had been basically white. The presbytery had suggested that

our black church from the inner city, which was called Tabor Presbyterian, merge with them. We were a totally black congregation. They had the wealth, and that was their church. They had the beautiful physical plant. We had many, many members. We had raised money for a new building. So we came over with the money we had raised, many, many members with terrible attitudes. This minister somehow brought this church together. He was such a gentleman. Everybody loved this man. He was in his 60s when he came. He stayed there about 20 years. When he left—he retired— everybody loved that man, and so much. The whites stayed there. They did not leave. And a few of them are still there. He is a wonderful man.

Mary says:

My philosophy of life is strictly one of giving of the best to the world and the best will come back to you. It's very simple. Do over? No, I think I've had a very good life. I think God has been very good to me. I've been very fortunate. I think I have exceeded the expectations for my life. I have received; I have given; I still have more to give; I still have more to receive. God has left me here, and he expects more from me, and I'm going to find out what that is. I'm going to do it; I'm going to do it to the best of my ability. And I'm going to get on and enjoy my life because that's what I'm here for.

(Note: Mary's interview was on October 25, 2007.)

Constance Hobson

This is a story about a skilled musician. Constance Hobson is that prodigy. She was born in Washington, DC on September 22, 1926. Constance's mother was from Canada, and her father was from West Virginia. Her mother's sister came to the US from Canada first. Then she sent for Constance's mother. They came to the US in search of better job opportunities.

Constance was an only child, but she grew up with cousins who were like siblings to her. The cousins were the children of her mother's sister. She lived on Vermont Avenue, NW in Washington between R and S Streets. She attended DC Public Schools. Her first junior high school was Shaw Junior High School. There came a time when Constance was about to go to the 9th grade that DC students were forced to go to the schools within their neighborhood boundaries, and Shaw was not her neighborhood school. Many of her classmates who were affected decided to go to Dunbar High School for the 9th grade rather than another junior high school. Constance wanted the experience of a 9th grade graduation from junior high school. She decided to go to Garnet-Patterson Junior High School.

At the time she entered Garnet-Patterson, Constance was already an accomplished pianist. She even attended the junior piano department at Howard University; and we can assume that at that time, the best African American music teachers in the country were there at Howard University. Well, one day, her principal at Garnet-Patterson called her to his office. Constance wondered what she had done wrong. It turned out that the principal wanted her to play the piano for him. Her principal enjoyed her music so much that almost every day she would play for him.

Constance became the regular pianist at school programs, and she also was pianist at her church. She did graduate from junior high school, after which she attended and graduated from Dunbar High School, which had a stellar reputation. Because of the segregated society at the time, the teachers there were overqualified, and they were dedicated to the students.

After graduating from high school, Constance studied music at Howard University, where she met her husband who was also a musician. Their marriage was to later end in divorce. She received a Bachelor's degree from Howard University and a Master's degree from Catholic University. After college she spent 36 years at Howard University as a professor of music theory. Some of her students who have become well known are Jessye Norman, Roberta Flack, Donny Hathaway, and Adolphus Hailstork. Constance has retired from Howard University, and she is Professor Emeritus, College of Fine Arts, Howard University. Although Constance has given away her grand piano, she still devotes time to music; she spends time cataloguing the work of the great musicians she has known so that their work will not be forgotten.

Now, Constance has been playing bridge since she was about 12 years old. When her family needed a fourth for bridge at home, they called Constance in. She remembers one humbling bridge experience when she was about 16 years old. She was the guest of a descendant of Frederick Douglas at Highland Beach, Maryland. Her hostess asked her if she played bridge. She proudly answered YES, and she sat down to play against two little old ladies. Well, those ladies gave her a serious bridge thrashing. They were well-known and respected leading bridge players. She said she thought twice about proclaiming her bridge prowess after that experience.

Tournament duplicate bridge came into Constance's life around 1989. She joined the Washington Bridge Unit at that time to be part of a team, which included some of the other ladies written about in this book. She speaks highly of the mentors of her team, the first of which was the late Charles Hanson, the husband of a team member. The second mentor was her team member, Jackie Thompson, who really helped sharpen the team's skills. She made sure that each team member could partner with the other three team members.

Constance traveled extensively to tournaments with her bridge team, including an international tournament in Trinidad in the Caribbean. Once, while vacationing in China, Constance and another WBU bridge player, Herb Quarles, attempted to play in a bridge club there. The club was restricted, and they refused to let them play.

Since joining the WBU, Constance also has been very active in officer, committee chair, and committee member positions. These positions include membership on the ABA's National History and Archive Committee and five years as Chair of the History and Archive Committee of ABA's mid-Atlantic section. Her favorite bridge personalities include many past and present WBU top bridge players who took the time to critique her play. Constance rarely plays bridge nowadays. Like her grand piano, she has just about given the game up. She says she has met the bridge goals she set for herself—to become a diamond life master in the

ABA, and to become a life master in the ACBL. She still maintains her membership in the WBU.

What does Constance do these days? She has been an active member of People's Congregational United Church of Christ for 50 years, even though she grew up in Metropolitan AME (African, Methodist, Episcopal) Church. She enjoys puzzles, and one of her greatest loves is traveling. The few places Constance has not visited include Australia and Antarctica. With her 94-year-old best friend Constance has traveled the highways and byways of the world. They enjoyed seeing places off the beaten path in their travels to really get to know the people and places. Once, they were so engrossed in their surroundings that they were locked inside a bank in Germany after its closing. (Note: Constance's best friend passed away about two weeks after this author interviewed Constance.)

Constance and her husband had one son who died a few years ago at the age of 41. He was attending an Omega Psi Phi fraternity convention in Atlanta, Georgia. Constance's philosophy of life is: Do your best despite obstacles. Live and let live.

(Note: Constance's interview was on May 17, 2007.)

Elizabeth and James Janifer

This is the story of James and Elizabeth Janifer. (They preferred to use the questionnaire to write their answers instead of my interviewing them.) At the time of their participation in March 2008, they had just celebrated their 64th wedding anniversary. They are quite a loving and devoted couple. They are very active, and they are trim and fit as a result. They are also hardworking. When the Washington Bridge Unit purchased its home in the late 1990s, Jim was instrumental in getting it into workable condition.

Jim Janifer was born November 15, 1919 in Washington, DC. He is from a large family, and his sister Dr. Mary Gross is also featured in this book. He enjoyed growing up in the city. He left when he joined the Army in 1942, and he returned to Washington after his retirement. Libby was born August 23, 1922 in Maryland. She grew up in New York City, and she liked it fine. Her parents and grandparents were Catholic, and she attended a Catholic elementary school. Jim went to school all over the world while he was in the Army. He received a Bachelor's degree from the University of Maryland, and Libby completed her Bachelor's degree in New York City.

The couple met at the USO (United Service Organizations) in New York City in 1944, and they were married in that year. Jim's career was with the US Army, and Libby refers to herself as an Army wife. Jim was in the Army for 25 years. They were happy to retire. The couple has a host of children, grandchildren, and great grandchildren. They have three children, five grandchildren, and four great grandchildren. They enjoy getting together with them. They have yearly family reunions. Currently, they attend a Baptist church.

Jim says they have been playing bridge since 1945. The couple has been playing bridge with the WBU since 1975. Libby's mother introduced them to both social and duplicate bridge. They apparently have played exclusively with each other as partner because they have exactly the same number of ABA master points. They also have played almost exclusively in the ABA, although Jim thinks a merger of the ABA and ACBL would be great. Their favorite bridge personalities are members of the WBU. They include grand life master, Reggie Chapman, Nanno Lee, Marion Best, and Herb Quarles. One of Jim's most memorable bridge moments was playing against Reggie Chapman. Libby's memorable moments include becoming a life master in the ABA. They have traveled out of town to bridge tournaments, but their favorite bridge locale is the WBU home, affectionately known as the Hut.

The Janifers have many things they do as hobbies and for relaxation. They go to their vacation timeshare approximately every three months. Libby enjoys frequenting the Poconos. They also go dancing often. Jim enjoys tennis.

He has been heard to say he would play more if he could find a 70-year old to take him on. His favorite books are law books and bridge books. Libby enjoys knitting, reading, crossword puzzles, and walking. She says Jim is her best friend.

Libby does not elaborate on racial and gender obstacles, but she admits to facing some in life. Persons whose lives she has admired are Martin Luther King, Jr., Harriet Tubman, Mary McLeod Bethune, and George Washington Carver. Libby's philosophy of life is the Golden Rule: Do unto others, as you would have them do unto you.

(Note: The Janifers submitted their questionnaire responses in March 2008.)

Helen McCormick

This is Helen McCormick's story. One word to describe Helen is energetic. Another is helpful. Whenever there is work to be done, Helen is there pitching in, and with a smile for everyone. Helen is hearing impaired, so she preferred to use my questionnaire as a guide to write answers to the questions, rather than have me tape an interview with her.

Helen was born in Washington, DC on March 22, 1925. She is a product of the Washington, DC public schools. In fact, she graduated as part of the famous Dunbar High School class of 1942. Helen and her husband grew up in the same neighborhood of Washington. They married in June 1946. Helen's husband passed away in 1988. She has two sons, a granddaughter, and two grandsons.

Helen received a BS degree from Minor Teachers' College and an MA degree from the University of the District of Columbia. Helen worked for the government from 1945 until 1950, but she always wanted to be a teacher. So, in 1950 she became a teacher. She taught until she retired in 1980.

Helen is enjoying her retirement years. She used to volunteer at DC schools. Now she teaches exercise to seniors and reads—a lot. Helen and other members of the Washington Bridge Unit regularly exchange books. Helen seems to be a prolific reader, because she exchanges an armful of books each week. Helen also enjoys walking. She is very trim. She says reading and walking are her favorite things to do. Her favorite authors are Danielle Steele and Deana Parker.

Helen belongs to Asbury Church where she brought up her sons. At church Helen ushers once per month, and she belongs to a birthday club.   One of her sons, his wife, and their two sons share a home with Helen. Helen once had a best friend, but she died in 1991. Helen takes regular vacations to the Outer Banks of North Carolina with her older son. She used to enjoy cruises, also.

We have not talked about Helen's bridge hobby. Helen started playing bridge in Winston-Salem NC, where she went for her honeymoon in 1946. The trip was a wedding gift from her husband's aunts. Her husband already knew how to play bridge, so Helen spent the week learning that new game. Later, Helen joined a social group that met once per month.

She started to compete in tournament duplicate bridge with the Washington Bridge Unit. She started playing with a WBU club that had games at 5:00 pm. This allowed her to play after work.   She especially remembers the large games the WBU held at the Banneker recreation center. She was fascinated with the champs who played there. She would watch them and try to play like them.

Helen's most memorable partner was Mabel Mosley who died of cancer about 15 years ago. They would often travel to ABA Summer National tournaments. Helen says she has had difficulty finding a regular partner for bridge vacations since Mabel passed. She loves bridge trips whether or not she wins points; and Helen was visible at the ABA Summer National in Detroit in July 2007. Locally, Helen loves playing at the WBU bridge home as much as possible. She plays on Tuesdays (sometimes twice), Wednesdays, Thursdays, and on weekends. As to playing bridge with the predominantly white ACBL, Helen says she has a problem finding a partner in that group. She thinks a merger between the two groups would cause travel problems because of the distance in reaching their local clubs.

One of Helen's greatest challenges has been hearing. Hard of hearing since 1947, she bravely underwent a serious operation in June 2006 to improve her hearing. She now hears much better with the help of an implant.

(Note: Helen submitted her questionnaire in May 2007.)

Naomi Millet

This is the story of Naomi Millet. She is a spiritual and reflective person. She also seems to quietly enjoy her time at the bridge table. Naomi is a native Washingtonian. Her birthday is November 15, 1923. Naomi was born on S Street NW between 10th and 11th Streets. That is near the church where she grew up. The home where she grew up was in the LeDroit Park section of Washington on U Street between 4th and 5th Streets. Naomi was the youngest of six children. She and one sister are left today. Even though she is her father's only child, her family never considered each other *half* brothers or sisters; they were all just brothers and sisters.

Naomi's father had two brothers in DC. Her family would visit the family of one of the brothers every week. Naomi attended Mott Elementary School at 4th and W Streets; Shaw Jr. High at 7th and Rhode Island; and Dunbar High School, which has moved from its original location.

Naomi says she attended racially segregated schools in DC, which affected the caliber of teachers she had. Back then if a black person graduated from Harvard, Vassar, Wellesley, etc., there was no place to work but teaching. So their teachers were highly qualified. Naomi thinks all of the schools prepared the students for college, whether they were academic, trade, or business schools. In fact, she remembers one of the smartest persons in college with her was from a trade school.

Naomi received her Bachelor's degree from Howard University. Since she was not wealthy and had no scholarship, she had to work all the way through college. Even though Howard was considered racially segregated, there were often Jewish people there and white people from other countries. Naomi remembers that the president of Howard University at that time, Mordecai Wyatt Johnson, would not allow the students to demonstrate to protest segregation. Howard was partially government supported, and the president thought it was more important to ensure those funds for new buildings and other scholarly needs. Naomi thinks she would like her grandchildren to attend a historically black university such as Morehouse today. She thinks African Americans can get something socially that they would not get from predominantly white universities.

Naomi attends the Baptist church that her mother and father attended. She grew up in that church. She married a Catholic. Although Naomi attended the Catholic church sometimes, she did not join it, but her children grew up in the Catholic church. Not only is religion important to Naomi, but also it *interests* her, and the older she gets the more it interests her. She says she has more time now to think about what she does not know about it. She began to study the Bible on her own, rather than just listening to sermons and going to Sunday school and Bible study classes. She is currently reading the Bible from cover to cover for the third time.

Naomi met her husband on the job. She was working as a cartographer at the US Department of the Interior. She received on-the-job cartography training there. She later became a mathematician, then a computer systems analyst. Naomi retired about 20 years ago.

She married her husband in 1947, and she is now a widow. Naomi and her husband have five sons and seven grandchildren, including a step grandchild whom she sees as no different from the other grandchildren. She also has one great grandchild who lives in Atlanta and is about two years old. All of Naomi's children live in the Washington, DC area, and she sees them often. Except for the grandchildren who live in Atlanta, Naomi also sees her grandchildren often. Naomi has lived in her house in a lovely section of northeast Washington for about 50 years.

Naomi enjoys visiting new houses that are being decorated for sale. She likes reading certain informational books, such as the *Da Vinci Code* or *Conversations with God.* In general, she gives her books away once she has read them. She will pick up a bridge book every now and then, such as Max Hardy's *Advanced Bridge Bidding for the 21st Century.*

That brings us to Naomi's passion—bridge. Naomi started playing bridge around 1960 when a coworker invited her and a friend, Juanita Mack, to come out to watch him play. He played with famous persons, such as Joe Henry.   Naomi and her friend went out to watch the coworker play. He invited them to join the Kings and Queens WBU bridge club. Then, they began to read bridge books together. They also went to tournaments where they would pick up a pair and play teams. Naomi went to Missouri to work for five years, and she and Juanita would meet for tournaments on their vacations.

When she returned from Missouri, Naomi and Juanita joined a team mentored by Charles Hanson. Up until then Naomi had no formal bridge classes, but Charles Hanson would lecture the team before every game. Naomi says that was when she got a good handle on bridge for the first time. Along with her teammates, Jackie Thompson, Muriel Hanson, Cornelia Proctor, Constance Hobson, and, occasionally, Jackie's mother, they would travel to different places to play.

Naomi remembers no particular racial problems while she played bridge. She says that they never attempted to socialize other than with each other. She does remember that back when African Americans could not play in the ACBL, one of the bridge greats, Mike Cappelletti and his wife, came to play at an ABA tournament. He was a friend of Juanita Mack, and he would talk to them from time to time at ACBL games after they became open to African Americans. Naomi's first partner was Juanita, but she considers her partnership with Jackie Thompson special because she was such a spectacular partner. You could rely on her always doing the right thing at the table.

She is not convinced that there is a good reason for an ABA/ACBL merger. She thinks the different master point structures in the two organizations are a barrier. Naomi has enjoyed bridge vacations, especially the international tournament she and her teammates attended in Trinidad. Her favorite locales for bridge would be places we do not go often, such as Oregon or Puerto Rico.

Naomi says she takes vacations, but they are not regular or planned long in advance. She is usually willing to go if someone wants to go somewhere, but if someone were to ask where she was going next summer, she could not say. She loves Mexico and has been there many times. She used to go to Puerto Vallarta in the summer. She says her money would go a long way, and it was enjoyable just doing nothing special. She would go out to dinner everyday, go to the beach everyday, and venture off where she could meet people.   She could see why Americans would want to retire there. She says people down there did not have just *one* servant; they might have one to open the gates, then one for different other things.

Naomi says her family has had one very nice family reunion. She says there are an inner family and an outer family, and they have to work harder on bringing the outer family in.

There have been more reunions on her husband's side of the family.

Naomi says everyone has challenges in life, and she has none she feels strongly about. She feels if one is secure in being black, racial obstacles do not bother them. She says if she were to do something over, it would be to get rich, but not for selfish reasons. She feels that with more resources she could help more people. She admires people who are rich and do more for others without a second thought.

(Note: Naomi's interview was on June 7, 2007.)

Thelma and Charles Nash

This is the story of Thelma and Charles Nash. They have been married since 1984. This is a second marriage for each of them. Thelma's first marriage was in 1952, and Charles' was in 1950. They were widow and widower when they met through mutual friends. The Nashes are a couple who complement each other very well. Charles is silent and reflective, yet assertive. Thelma is very spiritual, very articulate—always choosing the perfect word. She seems to have a flexible and intelligent mind.

Charles Nash was born on November 6, 1922 in Lake Providence, Louisiana. Charles says Lake Providence is in the northeast corner of the state near the Arkansas border. He grew up there and left when he was 18 years old to enter the Army. Charles says growing up in Lake

Providence was a joy to him. He could do anything he wanted. There was a big lake across from his home, where he could swim and play around. He also enjoyed playing baseball and other games. His family had a 97-acre farm, on which they grew all kinds of things, including nuts and fruit and cotton, also corn, wheat and oats. Charles says they had cows and horses and mules and tractors as well. They were always busy, and there was always something to do.

Charles is the third son of two older brothers and three younger sisters. Today, only one sister is living. Charles says they had good neighbors--Italians and Jews as well as blacks. He remembers when everybody was poor and you could leave your house wide open, and nobody was going to walk in without knocking. You did not have to worry about somebody taking anything, because you had nothing they could gain from you. He thinks morality was different, and people didn't hate each other. And everybody shared. Charles can remember when during the depression, white people would come and sleep at his house and eat food prepared by his mother, because they were a generous family. They always believed in sharing. They did have things to share. They had a big farm. There wasn't much money, but the farm was a livelihood. They were sure of being able to eat and sleep in comfort.

Although the neighbors were multi-cultural, the school system was segregated, like most in the South. There was a separate school for white people. Charles said the parish built a school for blacks in 1931. It went from 1st grade through 11th grade. That is the school from which Charles graduated.

When Charles graduated from high school at the age of 18, he went into the Army, where he served for five years. This was during World War II. He served in Australia, New Guinea, and New Hebrides. His unit landed in March of 1942, and they went into Townsville, Australia. From there, they went to Brisbane, then Port Mosby in New Guinea. There was lots of fighting in the area.   Most of the fighting was not in Australia. Charles attributes that to the Japanese homelands and graves in parts of Australia. The Japanese did only occasional bombing raids there.

Charles' unit was originally sent to do tank destruction. However, the equipment to do that never arrived, so they became an engineering outfit. They built temporary airstrips and bridges. Whenever something was cleared, the unit moved to another location. The unit also had men who serviced airplanes. Charles said that when the Japanese came over to bomb their area, the sky would be clear and sunny, but they sent so many planes it would become dark in the sky. His unit would move their planes from the airstrip and go up to engage the bombers. At night Charles' unit would fire on the enemy planes with antiaircraft guns. He recalls how hard it was to bring the enemy planes down; the antiaircraft guns would rock a plane, but not bring it down.

Charles said that although the aborigines were not integrated into Australian society, they were integrated into the Army. There were also aborigines from New Guinea who could be identifiably distinguished from those from Australia. General MacArthur was the supreme commander. However, Charles never met him because the general's headquarters were in Sidney, Australia. During his time in that part of the world, Charles did visit all the big cities in the area. He says that during the war Australia was not well populated. There were only 7 million whites on the continent. They only counted whites at that time.

Charles was in the Army from 1941 – 1945. After the war he migrated to the Washington, DC area, where one sister and one brother had settled. He had received a bonus, which the state of Louisiana gave to all the soldiers returning. Louisiana was the first state to give such a bonus, and very few other states gave bonuses. He married for the first time in 1950, and they had two daughters and one son. His son has since passed away. Charles' career began with the US Department of Treasury. Then he moved to the US Postal Service, from which he retired in 1970.

Thelma Boyd-Nash was born on March 17, 1924. The Bureau of Vital Statistics erroneously entered her birth date as March 15, and that is what is on her birth certificate. She was the third of three girls. She was born in Lancaster County, Virginia, in the northern neck of Virginia. It is the northeastern peninsula between the Rappahannock, the Potomac River, and the Chesapeake Bay. Her

family moved from Lancaster County to
Northumberland County when she was 4 years
old. Northumberland County is the
northernmost county on the peninsula. The
family moved because Thelma's father, a
Baptist minister, took a church in that county.

Thelma tells the story of how her father entered
the ministry. Before her father married her
mother, he was an oysterman. He and his
brother owned a boat, and they harvested
oysters for a living. After Thelma's parents
were married for about seven years and when
their first child was four years old, Thelma's
father told his wife he had been called to the
ministry. She told him that he could not be a
chair back minister--that he must prepare
himself.

Thelma's mother had graduated from Hampton
University in 1906, and she was a teacher. She
gave up her teaching job, and she went to the
local boarding high school to work as a
dormitory assistant and teacher, taking her
husband with her. This enabled her husband to
go off to Virginia Union University where he
prepared himself for the ministry. When he
finished, his wife returned to public school

teaching from which she would eventually retire.

Thelma's mother was her teacher in grades 1 to 3 in the one-room Howland School. Another of Thelma's many interesting stories is about the Quaker, Emily Howland, who founded the school. Thelma relates that Emily Howland came to the area to provide economic empowerment to freed slaves. Even though she was born at a time when higher education of females was discouraged, Emily Howland left the Quaker fold and was educated. She came to the Washington, DC area, where she taught at Minor School, later to become Minor Teachers' College, under Matilda Minor. She even took over for Minor when she left for health reasons. Subsequently, she worked in a contraband camp in what is now Alexandria, VA.

At the camp, Emily Howland was infused with the idea to work with the freed slaves. Since the 40-acres-and-a-mule promise never materialized for the slaves, she wanted to do something meaningful. Her father financed a land purchase for her to provide an opportunity for the newly freed slaves to own land. She found that land in the northern neck of Virginia.

Her first purchase was 317 acres. From that, she let the slaves exchange contracted work for parcels of land. So, the freed slaves purchased the land from her, worked the land, and became landowners.

During her second year in the northern neck area, Emily Howland worked with people in the area to set up a school. She allocated space for a schoolhouse, which was a church and school at the same time. They worshipped in the church on Sundays, and they held classes at other times—even in the evenings. People who were educated there went off to universities like Howard, Hampton, and Virginia Union. The community became a place where most of the people were landowners and they valued education. In addition to her early schoolroom, Thelma's father's First Baptist Church grew out of that schoolhouse.

Although Thelma craved an urban setting and often took her father to task about not accepting a church in a city, she loved growing up in Northumberland County, Virginia. Her father was a community leader, and he was an activist. Thelma says he was not just the preacher; he was the legal and financial adviser. He was a focal point of the community.

Both of Thelma's parents were active in the attempt to transform the community where they lived. Her father was local president of the NAACP. Many of the civil rights pioneers, such as Roy Wilkins, graced their home. Wyatt T. Walker, to become Martin Luther King's lieutenant, was a protégé of her father. Thelma's father was one of the community leaders who made sure the poll tax in Virginia was abolished. Her mother and her mother's young friends were the test cases for the equalization of teachers' salaries. So, during Thelma's youth, her community was very interesting.

Another item of interest is that during the Depression, Thelma's father built a brick church with a basement. It was like few other churches in a rural setting at that time. It was built without incurring any debt. A theologian from Union Seminary in New Jersey came through the region to do a book on black churches. He called it a cathedral in the woods.

Thelma graduated from Rosenwald High School in Northumberland, and at the age of 16 she went off to Hampton University. She never really lived at home again after that. She spent her summers off from college working in cities. In fact, after her first year of college, Thelma came home and told her parents she was going to Baltimore to work for the summer. Her parents told their 17-year-old daughter, no, she was not. Thelma told them she was going to pack. Her parents knew she had her own mind and would continue to challenge them. They gave in and found a way to get her to Baltimore.

Thelma appreciated most two things at Hampton. One was her orientation to college life course taught by Dr. Kenneth Clark. She said he challenged just about every assumption that was programmed into her being. At first, she was a little offended by what he said. She says as the year wore on, she realized what he was saying was another way of looking at things; and that course programmed her for the rest of her life. The second thing was the exposure to rich African-American music and great black musicians. The musicians on campus included Noah Ryder, Dorothy

Maynard, Marian Anderson, and Paul Robeson. Thelma resented being required to attend chapel at Hampton, but when she went, the glorious choir captivated her. She says the experience broadened her horizons. She says Nathaniel Dett was big there, and they used much of his work. In addition, the liturgical music from European sources completed the good mix of music.

Thelma graduated from Hampton in May 1944, and she found her way to a job in Prince Georges County, MD. Thelma says she could not get enough of the Howard Theater and the wonderful culture on U Street her first year in the area. As to work, she began a teaching career as a home economics teacher.

Throughout her career, Thelma continued to educate herself. For example, after her first year of teaching, she went to Morgan State University in Baltimore to learn about junior high schools. In 1950 she received a master's degree from New York University (NYU). She did this through attending classes in New York in the summers. Thelma had considered pursuing her graduate degree at the University of Maryland; but she knew entry into a graduate program there would require litigation to break the racial barriers. So like many black teachers of that period, she sought higher education in New York. At NYU the professor Max Wolf helped hone Thelma's critical thinking.

Thelma married the first time in 1952, and she has a son from that marriage. After maternity leave at the age of 34, Thelma cross-trained to become an English teacher. She received that certification through American University and the University of Maryland. About five or six years before she retired, Thelma received guidance counselor certification from Bowie State University. She also took courses at Howard University. Thelma's career was in education, but she worked as a home economics teacher, then as an English teacher, then as a guidance counselor. Thelma retired from education in 1975. She loved her career, but an eye problem made continuing very difficult.

Thelma's first husband passed away in 1979. Some time after his death, pursuing an interest in real estate law, Thelma took a real estate course at Prince Georges Community College. She took and passed the course for licensing, after which she did real estate sales for a while.

After their marriage in 1984, Thelma and Charles ran a trucking company for about 15 years. They continue to share interests such as, travel, bridge, and religion.

The Nashes say since their marriage and retirement, they have traveled just about everywhere they want to go. They've been to Africa, South America, Europe, and Asia. They have seen most of Western Europe, but they have been no further east than Austria in Europe. They love cruises. In Asia they did a cruise on the South China Sea. That took them through Tokyo and into Singapore. It also included China, Viet Nam, and Hong Kong. Thelma remembers it as a pretty intensive experience.

One of the Nashes' more recent cruises was a Greek Isle cruise, which included Istanbul, Turkey. Thelma found the Greek Isles fascinating, reminding her of Christian pioneer Paul's Ephesus experience. Thelma's daughter-in-law is from Morocco and they've had some fabulous vacations there. They have done Rome and Paris several times. Thelma says she would like to do Scandinavia; they have only visited

Denmark there. They have also traveled extensively in Canada and the Caribbean.

In January 2007, Thelma was diagnosed and treated for stage one breast cancer. Since then they have curtailed some of their traveling. But, they are getting back into it, with a California trip and a New York trip with Charles' granddaughter recently.

Thelma says her early family always took at least a summer vacation, which she considers an opportunity for renewal. Thelma says her first trip abroad was to Cuba. She and her first husband traveled there with close friends who were connected with the Cuban community. They spent over a week in Cuba hosted by friends of their friends. They spent most of their time in a resort-like community frequented by black upper class in Havana. Their host was the minister of education of one of the major provinces. They bonded with the hosts and remained friends for a long time. Their trip to Cuba was during the last political culture of Batista. Their hosts immigrated to the US after Fidel Castro's ascendancy into leadership.

Another early trip Thelma made was travel through Europe by Eurail with her son when he turned 13.

Thelma and Charles share an interest in bridge. Both are members of the Washington Bridge Unit. They are members of the WBU Duos club, and Thelma is a member WBU's Eastern Bridge Club. They play together in both clubs. Charles began to play bridge in 1953. He played as part of a group of about 12 persons. It started out as social bridge, then, it moved into duplicate bridge, still in the 1950s. Among the members of the group were WBU member Odele Mouzon and her husband. Mr. Mouzon knew more about bridge than the rest of the group; so he would instruct them when they made mistakes. That group broke up eventually. Charles recalls a 2-month vacation in Detroit, where the people seemed to play bridge all day. They drank coffee and played bridge. The coffee pot never appeared to go off.

Thelma began bridge more recently—within the last ten years. She had dabbled in bridge some, but she became really interested after Charles began to play again. He began because Rachel

Moore, an Eastern bridge club member, sought
a partner for a bridge newcomer. The
newcomer was Ethel Price who had come to the
Washington area from New Jersey. Thelma
suggested that Charles play. She knew he had
played in the past, and she thought he might be
interested. He agreed to be her partner, and
occasionally Thelma would accompany him to
the WBU home, the Hut, where she would
either observe or play. She became drawn into
bridge, and she began to take courses from
instructors at the Hut. Those instructors include
Bea (Elizabeth) Woods, Herb Quarles, Louis
Garner, and John Coleman.

Thelma enjoys bridge, not only because it is
challenging, but also because of the opportunity
to interact with other people. She says it is a
social situation, where you build a network
within the bridge group. She finds it both
interesting and fascinating. She enjoys the
social interaction with so many interesting
people gathered in different clubs at different
times.

Thelma says she regularly reads the bridge
column in the Washington Post. When she and
Charles go on cruises, they spend lots of time at

the bridge table. They are often on cruise ships. The cruises are not bridge cruises, but there has been a bridge instructor on almost every cruise they have done. Their last cruise was with a group of Europeans, and they played the European bridge system. The Nashes say the system was a little different from our systems and challenging, but they hung in there. They enjoyed the experience.

Thelma has a very perceptive description of bridge players at the bride table. She says:

> Just finding myself engaged in duplicate bridge is astounding to me. Seems to me most highlights of my life have been situations that I just kind of backed into. And I backed into bridge; and once there I find it absolutely fascinating. The personalities of many of the people whom I'd first met, later developed into people who were not the people I first met. The impressions changed dramatically as I played more and engaged more with them. Duplicate bridge players are very serious. When I first encountered them, I was a little apprehensive.

Some of the personalities rubbed me the wrong way because I thought, these people are very critical... But later on the more I played, the more I realized, they're not really critical. They're trying to help you with your game, and they want to improve their experience at the table. That wore off as I got to mingle more with the people. I did not see anyone in the situation who was offensive. They were themselves. That was a teaching situation for me. It was really enlightening because I'd not had that kind of interaction prior to the bridge experience, (in) so-called social situations.

Some memorable bridge personalities for the Nashes, in addition to bridge instructors, include WBU members. Rachel and Carrothers Moore play with them at home from time to time. They find the Moores very helpful and instructive even in that social setting. They consider Nanno Lee very gracious and helpful. Thelma was quite impressed with Ann Derricotte's skill when she encountered her at the table as a new player. She was amazed and thought, the lady really knows something. They have taken no bridge vacations, but they

have played locally in the WBU Cherry
Blossom tournament once or twice. Thelma
thinks if they could meld Charles' card sense
with the things she has picked up in classes and
bridge sessions, they might be a pretty good
team at the bridge table.

Religion is an integral part of the lives of both
Nashes. They are both Presbyterians now and
members of Sargent Memorial Presbyterian
Church. They both grew up as Baptists.
Charles learned to appreciate other religions
when he attended nondenominational services
when he was in the Army. He thought the
services were enjoyable because they taught in
ways different from what he was accustomed.
After leaving the Army he became a Methodist.

Thelma has what she calls a quest view of what
religion is. She considers religion a very
important force in her life, the center of her
being. Her quest keeps her constantly searching
for meaning. Even as a child Thelma, in a strict
Baptist household, suggested to her parents that
perhaps Catholicism was all right. One of her
readings, *The Power of Myth* by Joseph
Campbell, has contributed to her knowledge of
the origins of our modern understanding of

religion. She and Charles also took a class given by a Harvard professor on the meaning of God. She says we have to understand that Jesus was a Jew, and Christianity is what he did in his brief life. Thelma says when she works outside in the yard she is in contact with the Universal Creator. Her Universal Creator is constantly creating, and she co-creates with God.

Working in the yard is one of Thelma's fondest hobbies. She does all the landscaping, except cutting the grass. When I visited her beautiful premises prior to the interview, I found her trying to find a safe spot for a bird's nest filled with eggs that had been dislodged. When young people come by and see this 84-year-old working in her yard, they say, you can *do* this. She answers, yes, and you can too.

Thelma also loves to read. She has a vast assortment of books. Her current favorite reading is Taylor Branch's work. He has a trilogy: *Parting the Waters*, *Pillar of Fire*, and *Canaan's Edge*. The first book in the trilogy is a history covering civil rights during the Martin Luther King Years. WEB Dubois' biography by David Lewis fascinates Thelma.

Thelma has another hobby, which may be seen more as life work. She is a community activist, following in the paths of her parents. She says:

> My thinking is, every decision made at home or in the community, small or universal, is political. So I've always been curious about who is doing what, and why, as it can be discerned.

Thelma has belonged to the League of Women Voters since the 1960s. She also worked on the Prince Georges County Library Board of Trustees during the 1960s. It was during that period that most of the libraries in the county were built. The board chose sites, architects, furnishings, and many other related items. Thelma says she was very, very busy and very involved. Her work on the libraries actually led her to join the League of Women Voters to see how the overall process worked.

Charles' hobbies include pinochle and all kinds of card games. Thelma says he loves double deck pinochle. Charles says he does very little reading now because of vision problems. He thinks even the newspaper print has gotten smaller so they can save paper.

In addition to his two daughters, Charles has six grandchildren and four great grandchildren. Most of them live in the Washington area. He sees one grandson often. His best friend is now deceased. Charles says that since his parents passed away, his side of the family has not had reunions. When his sister and brother who lived in Washington were still living, he saw them at least weekly.

Thelma's son turned 50 recently, and he has a wife and an 18-year-old son. They live in New York. The son is a musician. He is a bass player and member of a band. He also teaches music in the New York City Public Schools. Thelma and Charles see them quite frequently. Thelma's very best friend has gone into Alzheimer's. She developed a second best friend, and she has gone into dementia. She has a close friend, Jan, whom she met on the job. Thelma and Jan have been very supportive of each other professionally and personally. Jan currently is instrumental in the promotion and application of the Comer process developed by Dr. James P. Comer of Yale University. She has become coordinator for most of his programs throughout the country.

Thelma has begun things to seed a family reunion with her relatives on both her parents' sides. Thelma's two sisters have passed away, but one of her sisters lived in their home community for the last 15 years of her life before she died in 1992. That sister kept Thelma in touch with her father's side of the family. In the summers they would gather in the setting of the church that Thelma's grandfather founded. She saw relatives and friends there whom she had not known, and she began to try to pull them together at later events.

Thelma had a big party of over 200 friends and family members last summer. One of the reasons for the party was to present Thelma's son's music. The family in attendance was from both her parents' sides. Their participation was partially driven by a book that Charles' nephew found. It was a book from the WPA (Works Progress Administration, then Works Projects Administration after 1939) slave writers' project. The writers talked to persons born in slavery and documented their stories. Thelma's grandfather on her mother's side was in the book.

Thelma interested her mother's side of the family in the book, and that common interest has helped seed efforts to bring together members of the family. Thelma got the DNA kit for tracing a family's ancestry, and she gave it to a male member on her father's side. She says she, herself, will also do a DNA test.

Charles' philosophy of life is about change. He says change will take place, and we will help it take place if we get tired enough of the status quo. He says he would not do anything over. He says if you regret what you did not do, you would probably regret it again if you tried to do things over. The persons he has admired most are his parents. His parents were respected in the community, and his father was a community leader. Everyone knew them. His parents were generous to all. His mother belonged to the same church all of her life. He also had an aunt whom he thought was terrific.

Thelma has two philosophies of life. The first is, we are all God's—the creator's—children; we are made in the image of God; and God is spirit. The second is, no one will define my humanity. Thelma tells a story about how she lived this philosophy. She says:

I go to Hampton on the bus my second year there; and I guess it was after the initial ruling about interstate travel on buses. And I got on the bus in my little village and sat on the second seat from the front and opened my book. The driver started off. He had not gone 5 miles when he stopped the bus, rose from his seat, and came back and stood over me. And said, 'You're sitting in the wrong seat.' My eyes were glued to the pages of my book. I didn't take my eyes off the book. I never looked at him. He said, 'I said, you have to move to the back.' I heard him, did not see him. He stood there for a minute or two, and then he said, 'this bus is not going farther than Warsaw. It's not an interstate bus.' I didn't move my eyes from the book. I was terrified! I can still get that feeling, remember it! He stood a minute longer and turned on his heels and went back to his driver's seat and sat. His neck was blood red. He drove that bus to Warsaw.

I told my parents, and my father said, 'Thelma, I don't want to come and get you out of jail.' I was scared, but I wasn't going to move. Because I had decided early on, that nobody on this planet was going to define my humanity. When I transferred at the bus station in Richmond, I'd go drink out of the white fountain. Luckily, nobody saw me and dragged me off in chains. I'd go into the white restroom but would not use it… And that has been my demeanor all my life, as far as I can remember.

In terms of doing things over, Thelma says she would do almost everything, and probably not do it any better. She says her life has been blessed; if one thing did not work for her one day, then there was always a gift. She says her parents are her heroes, and she admires the wonderful people in her early rural community. Other people she has admired are: Kenneth Clark, Howard Thurman, Thurgood Marshall, and Martin Luther King, Jr. Martin Luther King, Jr. is also her hero. She sees him as a reincarnation, a manifestation of the God force in our time.

(Note: The Nashes' interview was on April 30, 2008)

Ivy Nelson, Ed.D.

This is the story of Dr. Ivy Nelson. She is a real student—eager to learn. She is also generous. Ivy was born in Jamaica, West Indies in the city of Port Maria. Ivy has two birthdays. Her actual birthday is December 22, 1923. Her birth certificate shows December 29, 1923. Ivy has an amusing story about how that happened. Her mother delivered her with a midwife. She thought she had one week to get the birth registered, but as a single mother, she was not able to get the birth registered until two weeks after the fact. Since she thought she was late, she gave the officials the December 29 birth date. Ivy and her mother moved to Montego Bay, the capital of Saint James, Jamaica, when she was 13 years old. Ivy's mother was born in Saint James, and she thought the place would provide better opportunities for her only child.

Ivy attended public schools in Jamaica. Even though she won scholarships to private schools, it still would have caused a financial burden since her mother would have had to pay for a place for her to live. Her mother provided private lessons to supplement her public school lessons by doing laundry for teachers in exchange for the lessons. After graduating from public schools in Montego Bay, Ivy continued her education by attending nursing school. At the age of 26 with her nursing credentials in hand, Ivy moved to the United States.

In the United States Ivy first lived in Baltimore for one year. Even though she had registered nursing credentials from Jamaica, she was advised that she needed psychiatric nursing credentials to receive accreditation. She left Baltimore and went to work at the Crownsville Psychiatric Hospital in Crownsville, Maryland to obtain that accreditation. She was at Crownsville from 1951 through 1962. She made a lot of progress working there. She began as a staff nurse and moved up through head nurse and administration until she became head of the education department there.

In 1962 Ivy moved to Washington, DC to work in the school of nursing at what was then Freedmen's Hospital. She left DC in 1968 to teach at North Carolina Central University in Durham, NC. Ever thirsty for more education, Ivy moved back to Washington, DC in 1970 to earn a doctorate degree (an Ed.D). After receiving her doctorate, Ivy went to work at Federal City College (now part of the University of the District of Columbia) as Director of Nursing. That was in 1974.

Ivy retired in 1992. She says she might have worked longer but it hit her that she was 70 years old and she had been working since she was 15 years old.   She was not tired of working, but something told her it was time to stop. She had checked with her school's personnel department to see how much annuity she would have if she retired; and since she was eligible for social security, she decided she would have enough money to live on if she retired. Ivy said her main problem with retirement was she gave up some of her good habits, such as walking. She used to walk a lot, but she became afraid of the growing crime on the streets, especially drive-by shootings. She also used to sew and crochet, but she gave those up too.

Since religion has always been a central part of her life, Ivy did continue to go to church. She is a member of Sargent Memorial Presbyterian Church, where she teaches Sunday school and serves on several committees. She used to sing in the choir, also, but does that no longer. It was at church in 1992 that Ivy met persons who introduced her to the Washington Bridge Unit and competitive tournament duplicate bridge.

Ivy began playing bridge back when she worked at the psychiatric hospital in Crownsville. MD. The staff there taught her first how to play pinochle, then bridge. Always eager to learn more, Ivy would go to the library for books that helped her to learn more about bridge. So, in 1992 Ivy really got back into bridge. The bridge players at her church introduced her to the Eastern bridge club (part of the WBU) where she is now president.

Bridge has given Ivy many pleasant moments and many challenging moments. Ivy relates one amusing situation that shows how bids in bridge do not always mean what they seem to. Ivy and her partner were playing against a leading bridge player (Dr. Clarice Reid) and her partner. After one opponent's bid, Ivy's partner bid 2 no-trump. Ivy thought his bid meant he had a very strong hand, and with her good hand they could win all the books but one (6+6); so she bid 6 no-trump to contract to win those 6+6 books. Well, her partner's bid meant he had mostly clubs and diamonds. Since Ivy's side did not have much in the other two suits, they did not even come close to making their bid.

A regular and compatible partner is very important to regular bridge players. Ivy's first partner was a man from her church. He tried to help her improve her bridge game, but Ivy thought male dominance issues caused that partnership to suffer. She later had a long-term partnership with a lady named Ora Sidney. Their partnership lasted until Ora passed away. Ivy's current favorite bridge book is by a top national bridge player named Max Hardy. Today, Ivy is disappointed in the progress she has made in bridge. She thinks part of the problem is not having a regular partner. She still hopes to find one.

Ivy has never married. When she was young and still in Jamaica, a young man called on her mother to ask for Ivy's hand in marriage. That frightened Ivy because she did not want to get married at that time and she did not want to marry that young man. However, Ivy knew that if her mother accepted the young man's proposal, she would have to marry him. Her mother said no. Her mother realized there were many things that Ivy really wanted to do.

Although she has never married and had children, people like neighbors have always looked out for Ivy. She has had many, many friends who have been like family. She stayed in the home of a female bridge player from her church for many years. That person's oldest daughter petitioned her family to give Ivy their last name because she saw Ivy as family. Ivy says people have always trusted her with the care of their children. Another family-like friend for Ivy is a young man she met when she visited Nigeria. She helped the young man considerably when he came to the US to attend school. He now lives in the US and is doing very well. He wants to repay Ivy and lavish gifts on her. However, she encourages the young man to give, instead, to others who are in need.

Ivy has an adopted sister back in Jamaica who comes to the US often to visit her. In fact she was to attend the ABA's 2007 summer national tournament with her. Ivy also has other family-like friends in Jamaica, to whom she gave the house she had bought for her mother. Ivy's mother passed away in 1979. Before she died, she visited Ivy often here in the US, and Ivy wanted her to move with her over here. Her mother could not get used to living in a home with locked doors, so she preferred to live at home in Jamaica.

Ivy does not have a best friend. She thinks they violate confidences. Ivy likes bridge vacations, and she likes cruises. She is always looking for a cruise partner. She has enjoyed Mediterranean and Grecian cruise tours. She also enjoyed land trips to Greece, where she has been a lot. She has visited Hawaii three times— once as a working vacation. Her favorite things to do include games, such as scrabble and backgammon on the computer. She used to read a lot of novels by authors such as Danielle Steele, but nowadays she likes books that help her understand herself. An example is writings by Rick Warren whose question is, "Why Am I Here?" She finds that reflective.

If Ivy were to do anything over, if she had her druthers, it would be to become a parent. She is the parent of every child with whom she comes in contact. (It bothers her if people assume an ulterior motive for that.)   She considers the class system she grew up under in Jamaica more of an obstacle than racial obstacles. She considers paternalistic men, especially at the bridge table, a gender obstacle she has faced. Her philosophy of life is: Give something back of oneself. Of all the people Ivy has come across over the years, she admires her mother most.

In reflection, encouragement from others helped propel Ivy's work career. Part of Ivy's progress at Crownsville was because she was encouraged to get more education. Although the patients at Crownsville were not multicultural, the staff was. Three of the white nurses at Crownsville went to school regularly, and a white head nurse suggested to Ivy that she do the same. She was a little offended at first, but she decided to go to the University of Maryland to just take classes.

While Ivy was studying at the University of Maryland, the Dean told her that educational requirements for nursing were changing. Ivy then studied for a BS in nursing education, which she received in 1959. While she was still at the school, the dean of nursing told her he had money for good, qualified minority students. Ivy took advantage of that, and she received a master's in psychiatric nursing in 1960. She later studied at American University because she did not wish to have three academic degrees from the same school. At first she was paying her own way for doctorate studies at American. Then, an official there said the school had money for qualified students; and from then on the school provided the finances she needed for doctoral studies. So, in 1973 Ivy received an Ed.D. from American University in Curriculum and Support in Higher Education.

A final thought Ivy wants to share is that she would not be where she is today were it not for World War II. Jamaica was under British rule.

Britain needed nurses for the war. Britain gave money to its colonies for nursing training. Ivy received free nursing training in Jamaica because of that.

(Note: Ivy's interview was on June 15, 2007.)

Cornelia Proctor

Cornelia Proctor is a petite, youthful looking woman. She was born in Oakridge, Virginia, which is about 150 miles from Washington, DC. She was born January 17, 1920. She moved with her parents to Washington when she was two years old. She grew up with her two brothers and two sisters. She has just one brother and one sister left today. Cornelia is a product of DC Public Schools including Dunbar High School. She also has a degree from the University of the District of Columbia.

In terms of segregated versus integrated schools, Cornelia thinks the segregated schools of the past had some good points. For example, she thinks the teachers were more dedicated when she was in school. They made sure the students got a good education and were qualified. Students could go further if they liked. There were also vocational schools. She thinks they made a mistake when they eliminated vocational schools in DC. There are many young persons who cannot go to college, for financial or other reasons. Vocational schools offer them a choice.

In 1941 Cornelia married her husband Leonard. He was from Detroit. She met him through family friends in Washington. The marriage was short lived because he was killed in a jeep accident in Italy in 1946 after World War II. Although their marriage was short, it was happy. Cornelia has one son who lives in the DC area. Cornelia also had two grand children who died tragically. Despite that, Cornelia is blessed with lots of friends who keep in touch. Some of the friends are local, and some live out of town. She has lost many friends over the years but continues to acquire new ones. She is also close to her sister and brother who live in the DC area.

Cornelia had a long and interesting career with the federal government, first with the Department of Army, then with the Justice Department. At the Justice Department she worked on the personal staff of Robert Kennedy. She not only saw him everyday, but she met many movie stars who came through to see him, such as Peter Ustinov and Peter Lawford. She remembers Robert Kennedy's judicial reception at the White House while John Kennedy was President of the US. She met both Jackie and John Kennedy, as well as all the Supreme Court justices. Her job was a political appointment.

Robert Kennedy was about to become manager of John F. Kennedy's second presidential campaign when JFK was assassinated. Afterwards, she remained with the Justice Department in the Bureau of Prisons where she published the publication on national executions in the US. The files were quite interesting. She read background information on prisoners such as Al Capone. Later, during the early stages of computing, she became a computer analyst. Cornelia worked 30 years for the federal government. At the end of her 30 years, she retired.

Religion has always been very important to
Cornelia. She is a long time member of Saint
Gabriel Catholic Church. She belongs to the
Sodality organization for women in the church
there. The group boasts 100 members present at
each monthly meeting. The group is active in
raising funds for the church. Cornelia edited
the Sodality's monthly publication for many
years, but she has given that up.

Bridge is one of Cornelia's most enjoyable
pastimes. She plays party or social bridge at the
homes of club members. In fact, she is part of a
party bridge group that has met once per month
for over 50 years. In addition Cornelia has
played competitive duplicate bridge at the
Washington Bridge Unit and at tournaments
since the late 1980s.

Cornelia remembers the Baronites as the first
WBU club. It was named after Cecil Baron,
one of the founders of the ABA and the WBU.
In the early days the WBU games were held at
the Banneker Recreation center in NW
Washington. Because the WBU grew and the
center could not accommodate so many bridge
games, the WBU first rented space in Silver

Spring, MD, then in the 1990s purchased a bridge home just across the DC line in Mount Rainier, MD.

Cornelia remembers fondly her bridge team that played together in the 1990s. They went as a group to national tournaments and did very well. Their mentor was a man named Charles Hanson, who was a team member's husband. The team was affectionately called Charlie's angels. The team did very well for a long time until some members stopped playing.

There has been talk in recent years of a merger between the ABA and the ACBL. Cornelia is doubtful that a merger will happen any time soon. Many ABA players think they might be absorbed in the ACBL and lose their historical identity.

One of Cornelia's most memorable bridge vacations was at an international tournament in Trinidad in the Caribbean. One of her team members was from Trinidad, and she planned the vacation for them. The international procedures for playing were different in some respects from US only games. A person could not see her partner because a screen covered each player. If a player could not communicate in the common language, the person would draw a picture. The bids each player made went through a passage area. Only the cards, as they were played, were on the table. There were cocktails, coffee, and tea between bridge sessions. After the tournament the team member host took the team to see more of the island. They were also treated to a stay in a luxury villa in Tobago.

Mahjong is another pastime that Cornelia has taken up lately. She learned it at a local senior center. She finds that she is now doing more mahjong than bridge. She finds it challenging and enjoyable. Since learning it at the senior center, she plays with three different groups made up of friends she met at the senior center. They play seriously for small amounts of money. No one ever loses more than $4.00. Cornelia explains that mahjong used to be mostly a gambling game for men in Asian countries. Her mahjong friends are all black women. Usually a group of 5 meets in a home. Four of the five play at a time. The fifth person allows each player to take a rest. The players bring their own lunch, and the hostess provides beverages.

Cornelia is a member of the Delta Sigma Theta sorority. Although she is not as active with the group as she used to be, it still keeps her busy. She has a golden life membership. Cornelia no longer takes regular vacations, but she has traveled extensively. She has been to Europe, Mexico, and Canada. She says she has not visited the Far East. She did go on a Christmas cruise last year. When her son was in the Navy, he was stationed in Sicily. She visited him there and loved it. She also enjoyed Rome, the Vatican, and Hawaii.   In addition to her pastimes and travels, Cornelia enjoys reading, both fiction and non-fiction. She reads something just about every night.

Cornelia says the following when reflecting on challenges and obstacles:

> There was prejudice during my working years, not in schools. Often, whether qualified or not, we did not have an opportunity. It really was unfair because they would give you all kinds of excuses, 'No longer have that position.' I am glad to see some of those barriers gone and more opportunities for young people. A

wonderful thing! They can compete on all levels.

The Golden Rule summarizes Cornelia's philosophy of life: Live the way you will always be proud of, and treat your friends as you would want them to treat you. As far as doing things over, Cornelia says she might have gotten her college degree earlier. She went to college after she retired from her government service. She thinks it might have made a difference in her working career. But, she did it for her personal satisfaction.

Cornelia's grades in college were better than those of some of the younger students. They had so many other interests, and some did not take school as seriously as they should. She wishes our young people would follow the Asian way of thinking, because those kids excel in all the top universities. Our kids could do that, but of course they have other interests, and think the opportunities will not come their way; but it will if you give yourself time. Years in school are very short, but you have the rest of your life to do all these things.

Cornelia says, "I have had a good life, in spite of all the tragedies and other things. I've been able to overcome them and keep moving. All these things are a part of life, and you have to accept them whether you like them or not. Keep moving."

(Note: Cornelia's interview was on May 1, 2007.)

Nora Tucker, Ph.D.

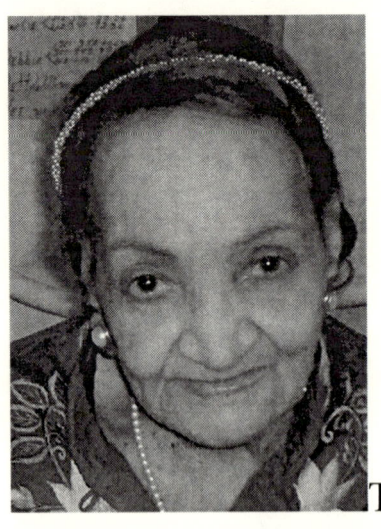

This is the story of Nora Tucker. You will discover that she is a very determined and very intelligent person. Nora was born in Newport, Tennessee on June 10, 1917. She was the only child of Myrtle and John Rasby. Her parents moved to Washington, DC first, and later they sent for Nora. She stayed with her grandmother in Tennessee before her parents sent for her. She also spent the summers with her grandmother.

The sisters of Nora's mother began teaching her the card game bid whist when she was about four years old. They gave her books to read and showed her how to do things with cards. The three aunts, who were all teachers, let Nora play cards with them when they came home from work. One of Nora's aunts founded the school she attended in Tennessee.

When Nora was in the 8th grade, she moved to Washington to be with her parents. At a young age Nora entered Dunbar High School in Washington, DC. She attended Dunbar for grades 9 through 12. At Dunbar there was a break room where the students could go between classes. It was there that Nora began to play bridge. A teacher taught her and others bridge by showing them the transition from bid whist to bridge. During that time Nora and her parents lived first near 6th and R Streets, NW, which was near the restaurant Nora's father owned on 7th Street, NW. Then, they lived on Harvard Street, NW. Nora also traveled extensively with her parents and her aunts. They went all over the world.

After graduating from high school, Nora entered Howard University at the age of 15. Nora's Aunt Rose who was a member of the Delta Sigma Theta sorority told Nora that she, too, must become a Delta. Following her aunt's command, Nora began playing bridge in the Delta room in the women's dormitory. Nora did not live in the dormitory at Howard

University, but she was there a lot because her Harvard street home was just around the corner from the Howard University campus. They would have bridge tournaments at Howard University, where they played for pennies, candy, cookies, or whatever. While she was a student at Howard, Nora invited younger kids to come to her home so that she could teach them bridge. Nora sometimes played cards at night with her father.

When Nora was a junior at Howard University, she met Percy W. Tucker. He saw her across the campus yard, and he asked to meet her. He was from Massachusetts, and he was a student at West Virginia State University. Well, when Percy asked to meet Nora, a young man brought him across campus to meet her. She told him she had to go; but he encouraged her to go for a cup of coffee. Nora agreed, and they went to a restaurant on Georgia Avenue near the campus, where she had a coke.

Percy walked her home, then he came back to meet her parents. He told her he did not want to go back to his school. He did go back to West Virginia State to arrange a transfer to Howard University. He accomplished that, and moved back to the men's dormitory at Howard. Nora says he looked at her, and she looked at him, and it was love at first sight. Later that year they got married. They were both juniors at Howard University. They kept the marriage a secret for a year.

 Nora and Percy both got jobs with the federal government after graduating from Howard University. Nora was an economist with the US Department of Labor. She headed a whole unit and taught many people, black and white, their jobs. She was one of the first blacks in the Labor Department, and she was written up in the newspapers for bringing in more black persons. She worked first in the Women's Bureau, then, in the Bureau of Economic Analysis. She retired from there after 32 years. Nora says her family did very well economically.

Nora and Percy were married fifty years when Percy died. They had three children—two sons and a daughter. Their son, David Richard Tucker, died in an accident in later years, but he left a daughter, who also has a daughter. So, Nora is a great grandmother. Their second son is Lance Tucker. Nora's daughter is Laurel Tucker Carter, and she has a son, Kip.

Nora says she always felt if she wanted something she would get it. She wanted a Ph.D., and she got it. In fact, she received a Bachelor's and a Master's degree from Howard University. Then she earned the Ph.D. in economic history from both Howard and American Universities. Nora says the Ph.D. degree helped her obtain high-level positions, where she could participate in planning sessions.

Further, Nora wanted her daughter to get a Ph.D., and she did, in sociology. Nora's daughter and her daughter's husband received Bachelor's degrees from Howard University. Nora's daughter teaches at the University of the District of Columbia. Nora says there is very little of her family left; so they do not have family reunions. In addition to her family, her best friends today are Geneva Wade and Elizabeth Woods.

Nora's bridge experience began early and continues today. She joined the WBU in the early days, when it was called the Washington

Bridge League (WBL). She remembers that a group of men had a club, which included Dewey Carr and Caesar Barron. Nora and other women formed a WBU club. That club grew out of a women's social bridge club, which included very young women as well as older women. Nora would like to acknowledge her bridge partners over the years, and we list many of them below:

Clarice and Art Reid, Ed Peterson, Dewey and Iris Carr (close friends of Nora and her husband), Mazaline Baird, Mildred Anderson, Faye Burke, Lucille Chenault (Nora's favorite bridge partner), Caspar Chappell (a good friend of Nora's husband); Gertie Coleman, (Gertie and John would come over and visit.); Shirley Craig, Lula Dawson; Sam Dendy, Audrey Dickerson; Regena and Winston Edwards, Rose Ann Elliot, Barbara Falls, Lloyd and Mary Farrow, Jeanette Felton (a very good friend), Gerrie Flowers, Barbara and Lou Garner, Alice Johnson, John Jordan (a favorite partner who taught her a whole lot); Carrolena Key, Eartha King, Florence Lindsay, Sally Lipscomb, Helen McCormick, Doris Mitchell, Reggie and

Jewell Chapman, Doris and Joe Payne, Vivian and Herb Pelham, John Phoenix (like a play brother, played all the time), Herb Quarles, Florrie Robertson, Dr. Ted Shell, Marie Smith (a favorite player), Hilda Thomas, Geneva Wade, and Bettye Whitney.

Nora says she likes both the ABA and the ACBL—she just wants to play bridge. With respect to a merger between the two groups, Nora said that was tried once. She said Dewey Carr got them all together. It worked for a little while, but not for long. Elderly people did not want to travel so far to play bridge. Her favorite bridge locales include Kansas City, Florida, and California. She traveled to all the cities that hosted tournaments, and she knew bridge players from all over. Bridge clubs across the country would have tournaments; they would spend the weekends there; and they would have so much fun.

As we stated earlier, Nora traveled all over the world with her parents and aunts. She also traveled extensively with her husband. They also covered the world. They especially enjoyed the islands, California, and Bermuda.

For years they rented a beach home at Highland Beach, Maryland. When Nora was a child, she received a camera, and that began her taking pictures all over the world. She was a great photographer. She has pictures she has taken of kings and queens. The husband of a very dear friend worked for the US Department of State. The State Department sent him to England, and Nora accompanied him and his wife. They met Queen Elizabeth, Princess Diana, and other royal family members. Nora says she met the entire court.

Nora has other hobbies besides bridge. She loves to read, novels especially. She also loved to skate. She says she was one heck of a skater. She used to roller skate up and down.

Religion has always been important in Nora's life. She says when she was with her grandmother in Tennessee, that was all she ever did. She had to teach religion to younger children. Her home church is Saint Luke's Episcopal Church in Washington. She has worked in the church everywhere she was needed. She taught in the church for a long time.

Travel comes up often when talking to Nora. She says travel is difficult now. The challenge is flying. She says she used to love to fly. She and her husband used to fly all the time. She would fly also with her bridge buddies, Faye Burke and Jeanette Felton. She says, "but not anymore." Her last flight was to Puerto Rico, and she says she was so afraid of that airplane. That brings us to what she would like to do over. Nora says she would like to live a little longer, of course; but she would like to see all the places she has been again. She has been all over the world; but she would love to see it again.

Nora has a philosophy of life. She says it is to help people, to push African Americans up. She says as a southerner she knew we had to be pushed up given the racial conditions in the country. Nora has also admired a few persons over the years. Two persons she admired are President and Mrs. Bill Clinton, whom she knew personally. She would have lunch with them and visit them at the White House. She also admired President Franklin D. Roosevelt.

She holds Mordecai Wyatt Johnson, the first African American president of Howard

University, in very high regard. His daughter was one of Nora's good friends.

(Note: Nora's interview was on December 10, 2007.)

Juanita Watts

This is the story of Juanita Watts whom you will find to be a determined, hardworking super-achiever. Juanita was born in Atlanta, Georgia on April 4, 1924. She had two brothers and one sister, none of whom is living now. She grew up in Atlanta in the same neighborhood as Martin Luther King, Jr. In fact, she teased her brother about being part of the MLK gang. She enjoyed growing up in Atlanta even though her parents were strict. She thinks that was because segregation was the law of the land, and her parents wanted to keep their children out of trouble.

When Juanita graduated from high school, she received a two-year scholarship to Spellman

College. Juanita was always industrious, and she worked in the summers. After her freshman year of college, she worked in a dining room in downtown Atlanta. She says she learned how to serve tables, and she got good tips because she did her job well and got along with everyone.

At the end of Juanita's sophomore year of college, Pearl Harbor had been bombed. This triggered the start of World War II. Always on the alert for opportunities, Juanita heard of a recruiting effort for college seniors to work for the government in Washington, DC to support the war effort. The recruiters were not at her college; they were at the neighboring Morehouse College. She asked a friend who had two sisters graduating about the recruitment effort. That friend could not help her. So, Juanita took it upon herself to go over to Morehouse to see the recruiters. She told the recruiter that she only wanted to work for the summer. He said they would pay her transportation to Washington, DC and her room rent while she was working. He said if she did not stay, she would have to pay them back when she left.

Juanita says that everything went smoothly for her getting the job. She even got her father's blessing, which was critical. She began work as a GS 2 for the US Army. When she arrived in Washington, the recruiters had arranged for the recruits to live in a dormitory at Howard University. That worked out fine for Juanita. She transferred to Howard University and continued to work while she was a student. Juanita has been in the Washington, DC area ever since that time.

Juanita met her husband at Minor Teachers' College in Washington, DC, and they married while she was still in college. Her husband was a student at Minor's who had just been discharged from the Marine Corps. He was a native Washingtonian, and he had interrupted his studies to join the Marines. This was over the objections of his parents. Juanita says her husband was a person who wanted to go where *he* wanted to go.

Juanita and her husband had one son. She now has one grandson and four great granddaughters. Juanita visits with them as often as she likes. Tragically, Juanita's husband and son both died from sarcoidosis, which afflicts the males in the Watts family. They generally are stricken with it and die when they are fairly young. Even the two sons of her husband's brother died from the ailment. (Her husband's brother died in a car accident.) Juanita was widowed in 1986. She says it is a challenge for her to encourage her grandson to take care of himself to avoid the family illness.

Juanita learned about bridge through her husband and his friends. She would play with them often. After she retired in 1984, she wanted to play with a group. She, then, joined the Washington Bridge Unit. In fact, Juanita served two terms as president of the WBU. She was president when WBU purchased its bridge home called the Hut. Juanita says in her early days of bridge, she went to most of the tournaments, both local and away. When someone said, "let's go," she was ready to travel. WBU member, Norma Vincent, is Juanita's favorite partner.

Juanita started with the Army as a grade GS 2 when she was in college. When she retired in 1984 after 42 years service, she had attained the highest level in the Senior Executive Service. When she retired, she was Director of the

Office of Small and Disadvantaged Business Utilization, Office of the Secretary of the Army. During her years of service, not only did she make tremendous progress on the job, but she advanced in education and training.

Juanita received a Bachelor of Arts degree from Howard University. In addition to her many certificates of achievement, Juanita completed the Federal Executive Development Program and the Program for Senior Managers in Government at the John F. Kennedy School of Government at Harvard University. One of her proudest achievements was being chosen as the guest speaker at the Martin Luther King, Jr. memorial service at Fort Ord, California in January 1984.

Juanita has traveled extensively. One special vacation she enjoyed soon after she retired was a trip to the Middle and Far East. She went to China, where she climbed the Great Wall of China. She has a certificate to commemorate that feat. Juanita says she and her traveling companions were treated like royalty in China. They were served at the same dining room table where President Ronald Reagan had been served.

Today, Juanita is active in her church, which is
Ebenezer United Methodist Church. It is in
Prince Georges County Maryland. It is not to be
confused with Ebenezer United Methodist
Church in southeast Washington, which is
where she and her husband married. That
church is the church of her husband's family.
Juanita was president of the United Methodist
Women for ten years. That group founded a
summer camp for girls, with which Juanita
worked. She now works with the scholarship
committee. Scholarships for students are a
cause dear to her heart. In addition to church,
Juanita is active in many organizations. They
include the Howard University Women's Club.
Juanita says she loves to read, but she does not
read as much now as in the past.

There are many persons whom Juanita has
admired over the years, including professors at
Spellman College and Howard University,
whose names now escape her. (Juanita lost
many of her papers and records in a flood at her
home.) With respect to obstacles in life or
education, Juanita admits that she was
fortunate. She worked very hard, but she
remembers a white female supervisor at work

who helped her. When the supervisor found out that Juanita was a student, she would let her leave early from her 4 pm to midnight shift so that she would have time to study. Juanita says the supervisor was from Tennessee and helped her despite the segregationist practices of that time. Asked if she prefers segregated schools to integrated schools, Juanita answers, sometimes I say yes, sometimes I say no. She said her kids, grandkids, and great grandkids went to integrated schools, and they got through all right.

Juanita's philosophy of life is The Golden Rule: do unto others, as you would have them do unto you. She says there is nothing she would do over. She finds a way to get along with people if she sees they might be difficult; and if she can avoid contact with them, she does.

(Juanita's interview was on May 9, 2008.)

Elizabeth Woods

This story is about Elizabeth Woods. Her story shows that she was a very determined and very industrious person. Even today she is one of the hardest working persons in the WBU; and she has received awards honoring that hard work. She was born in Columbus Georgia on October 25, 1925, the baby of six children. Elizabeth's father died when she was nine months old. Later her mother and her mother's mother moved the family to Pittsburgh Pennsylvania. Although Elizabeth loved her family, she did not like growing up in Pittsburgh. That was because of the health environment resulting from the steel mills. It was a very dirty city. There were many deaths from tuberculosis even among the young people.

Elizabeth was an honor student throughout her time in Pittsburgh public schools. She experienced few racial problems. Her high school graduating class of 200 had about 20 African Americans. The general feeling was that so few blacks were of little concern. The neighborhood where she grew up was integrated and predominately Jewish. She had good strong teachers there. Elizabeth found out recently that Lou Garner, another WBU bridge player, grew up right down the street from her and went to the same schools. She did not remember him at first because he was about ten years her junior.

Elizabeth attended West Virginia State College, and she received a Bachelor's degree from there. Although they were not a couple there, Elizabeth met her future husband at West Virginia State. He lived in Charleston, WV.

Elizabeth worked and saved money for college. She first worked in a job in a pants factory that paid $16 per week. When the opportunity became available, she switched to a government job in Pittsburgh that paid more money. She saved enough for college. However, after two years of college, she realized her money would run out in another year. At the time she worked for the registrar. His office was right next door to the dean. One day, she bravely approached him to ask if she could take some required courses at the same time that she took prerequisites. The dean informed her that there was a reason for prerequisites. Elizabeth explained that she would be forced to leave school early because her money could not take her through four years. The dean relented and let her take prerequisite and required courses at the same time. She graduated in three years magna cum laude.

In another brave act Elizabeth struck out on her own for Washington DC in 1948. Elizabeth had taken the US Civil Service examination for entry into the federal government while she was in West Virginia. She went home, and while she waited to be called, she made herself three dresses. When she was called after two weeks, she moved to Washington where she lived in Slowe Hall, a women's dormitory at Howard University. The beautiful black women there and their beautiful clothes impressed her. One

of the women took her under her wings. She
even took her to Connecticut Avenue to
purchase clothes, but Elizabeth found the stores
too expensive. She also met a person from her
Pittsburgh hometown in the dormitory.

Elizabeth began playing bridge while she was a
sophomore at West Virginia State. In order to
spend time with a young man she was dating at
the time, she would watch him play. While
living in the Slowe Hall dormitory at Howard
University, Elizabeth knew one person, Eartha
King, who played duplicate bridge. Eartha was
also from Pittsburgh. Elizabeth took lessons at
Banneker Recreation Center and played social
bridge for several years, after which she began
playing duplicate tournament bridge. She was a
founding member of the Banneker WBU bridge
club. That was approximately in 1970.

Elizabeth's main bridge partners were Geneva
Wade, Elizabeth Taylor, and Thelma
Whitehead. She recalls how exciting it was
when she and Geneva won first place in an
ABA Nationwide game one year. Elizabeth's
husband played a little bridge, but his busy
schedule did not allow him to pursue it
regularly. He was a member of the Columbians

WBU club. She traveled quite a bit for bridge tournaments in the early years, first with her husband then with her two regular partners. Her favorite bridge locale is Atlanta, GA. That is also the hometown of her parents' families.

Elizabeth's husband came to Washington DC to study pharmacy. They re-met, and they were married in 1949. She was widowed in 1986. They have a son and a daughter. Her son was valedictorian in both junior and senior high school—Taft Jr. High and Roosevelt High in DC. He and his wife graduated from MIT and earned Masters degrees from Stanford University. Since her son's public school career had been in predominately black environments, Elizabeth encouraged him to compete for admission at the mainstream universities.

Elizabeth's son has one son and one daughter. Her daughter has a daughter about the same age as her female cousin. The two granddaughters are the same age, and they are currently in college, and the grandson is in high school. Elizabeth taught all three grandchildren to play bridge, but only the grandson has pursued it. He plays during his free period at Thomas

Jefferson High School in Arlington, Virginia where he excels.

Elizabeth has always had a lot of faith in God and Jesus Christ. When she was growing up in Pittsburgh, church was the main community entertainment. She was a Methodist, and they would spend all day in church on Sundays. She also taught Sunday school. She later joined the Baptist church that her girlfriend attended, against the wishes of her family. Her husband was the son of a Methodist minister. After she came to Washington, DC, she and her husband would attend the chapel at Howard University. In fact, that is where they were married. When they moved to far northeast Washington after marriage, they began attending Sargent Memorial Presbyterian Church. She discovered that the husband of a girlfriend was pastor there. Elizabeth still goes to church there, where she has been a deacon. Her children were reared in that church also.

Most of Elizabeth's career was with the DC Public Schools. After five years with the federal government she left to become a teacher with the school system. But, the transition was not smooth. Her field was business, but her

college transcript showed no typing class.
Despite her proficiency as a typist on the job,
the DC school system would not hire her until
she made up the lack of typing on her transcript.
So she took a basic typing correspondence
course. She taught business for five years at
Langley Jr. High School, which is now a charter
school. She followed those years with 16 years
as a guidance counselor. Over the years
Elizabeth received a Master's degree from
Catholic University and more than 30 additional
credits at Maryland University. She retired in
1980 when her husband became ill.

Nowadays, Elizabeth's main hobbies are
playing and teaching bridge. She is a member
of the AKA (Alpha Kappa Alpha) sorority, and
she does community outreach at the AKA
house. This has involved voter registration and
bridge teaching among other things. She used
to read a lot, but she reads less now because of
eye trouble. Her husband's family has had
family reunions. Her sister who married into a
large family would extend participation in their
reunions to Elizabeth's family. Otherwise, she
remembers one reunion on her side of the
family, and it was enjoyable. About two weeks

before this interview, Elizabeth was matron of honor at her best friend's wedding.

Elizabeth reports as a main challenge her decision to leave Pittsburgh and strike out on her own for an unknown city. She considers two racial incidents as other challenges. While at Catholic University and the only black person in the class, the professor would call the roll and omit Elizabeth's name. When she raised her hand to inform the professor she was there, the professor replied, "I see you." Well, Elizabeth made sure the teacher saw her everyday because she always raised her hand to participate.

The second racial incident happened while she was in Pittsburgh. There was an eating establishment in Pittsburgh, where people were served at a counter. Someone told her that the establishment had a really nice restaurant upstairs. So, she and mainly female friends went there to eat. While they were leaving, the manager told her they would prefer if they did not come back. When she told her friends, most of them did not want to go back. She sought out her alderman and told him about the situation. He said he thought the manager stated the request such that they were not actually barred. He said they should go back, and see what happened. She and a few friends (mainly males, this time) went back. The manager was clearly bothered, but he refrained from saying anything.

A most memorable person in Elizabeth's life was a boarder in her mother's home who was like a member of the extended family. When Elizabeth was preparing to go off to West Virginia State College for the first time, her family had little or no help for her. The boarder, whom she considers an uncle, gave her an old suitcase that had to be secured with a rope. Elizabeth was very happy to have it. When she came home after her first year at college, the uncle gave her a brand new footlocker. He said he felt bad about the old suitcase he had given her. In addition, he sent her $5 per week the whole time she was in college. Years later when Elizabeth and her husband bought a new house for her mother, the uncle still lived there. Even after her mother passed away and two new generations lived in the house, the uncle remained.

Elizabeth's philosophy of life includes: look on the positive side; the cup is half full, not half empty. She believes, if you cannot say something nice to a person, say nothing.

(Note: Elizabeth's interview was on June 14, 2007.)

Appendix

A. American Bridge Association (ABA) Structure

- National Office
  - Sections
    - Eastern
    - Great Lakes
    - Mid-Atlantic
      - WBU
      - ...
    - Midwestern
    - Northwestern
    - Southern
    - Southwestern
    - Western

B.   Questionnaire

Questionnaire Groupings
•Bridge
•General background
•Family
•Education
•Hobbies and relaxation
•Challenges and obstacles

Bridge
1. How did you get started playing bridge?
2. How did you get started with duplicate bridge?
3. Where were you when you started bridge?
4. Where were you when you started duplicate?
5. How long have you been playing bridge?
6. How long have you been playing duplicate?
7. What are some memorable bridge moments?
8. Who are some favorite bridge personalities?
9. Do you prefer ABA, ACBL bridge, or both?
10. What are reasons you care to share for your preference?
11. Tell me about your most memorable bridge partners.
12. What do you think of a merger between ABA and ACBL?
13. Have you faced any racial obstacles in bridge?
14. Do you take bridge vacations?
15. What is your favorite bridge locale?

General Background
    1. Where were you born?
    2. What is your birth date?
    3. Where did you grow up?
    4. How did you like where you grew up?
    5. What brought you to the DC area?
    6. How long have you been in the DC area?
    7. Have you ever been married?

8. Are you married now?
9. How did you meet your spouse?
10. How long have you been married?
11. Do/did you have a career?
12. Were you happy to retire?
13. How does religion fit into your life?

Family
1. Do you have children?
2. Do you have grandchildren?
3. Do you have great-grandchildren?
4. Do you see your children often?
5. Do you see your grandchildren often?
6. Do you see your great grandchildren often?
7. Do you have a best friend?

Education
1. Where did you go to school.
2. What is your highest level of education?
3. Were there obstacles to getting an education?
4. Did you attend racially segregated schools?
5. Did you attend racially integrated schools?
6. Which do you prefer?
7. Which would you prefer for your children, grandchildren, or great grandchildren?

Hobbies and Relaxation
1. Do you take regular (yearly, etc.) vacations?
2. Where do you like to vacation?
3. Do you have other hobbies (besides bridge)?
4. What are your favorite things to do?
5. Who are your favorite authors?
6. What is your favorite book?
7. Do you have family reunions?
8. How often?

Challenges and Obstacles
1. Have you had challenges in life that you want to share?
2. Have you faced any racial obstacles in life?
3. Have you faced obstacles due to your gender?
4. Do you have a philosophy of life?
5. Is there something you would like to do over?
6. What person(s) have you admired most in life

Printed in the United States
204912BV00001B/394-498/P